MW00399163

The Art & Science of Resort Sales

BEN GAY III
Salesman • Speaker
Sales Trainer • Consultant

Voice: **(800) 248-3555**
(530) 622-7777
Fax: (530) 295-9337
E-Mail: bfg3@directcon.net
WWW.BFG3.COM

P.O. Box 2481
Placerville, CA 95667-2481
USA

© 2006 by Ben Gay III & The LJR Group, Inc.
All right reserved under International and Pan-American Copyright Conventions.

This publication may not be reproduced, stored in a retrieval system, or transmitted in whole or in part, in any form or by any means, electronic, mechanical, photocopying, recording, or otherwise, without the prior written permission of the Copyright owner.

ISBN 0-942645-07-3

**Library of Congress
Catalog Card Number: 89-82586**

Printed and manufactured in the United States of America by The LJR Group, Inc./P.O. Box 2481 Placerville, California 95667-2481
530-622-7777

TABLE OF CONTENTS

Preface

The sole purpose of this book is to assist *any* sales person to be more *successful* and *professional.*

The basic and advanced sales principles and techniques that are demonstrated throughout this entire book have been applied for the sale of the major types of *resort vacation properties.* However, with *slight* alteration and modification, these same sales principles and techniques can be applied just as effectively for selling *any product,* especially *big ticket items.*

In order to communicate properly, the author and reader must speak the *same* language. Therefore, a lexicon of words as they apply to sales and sales training, is listed *first.* A review of these words *before* reading the text is recommended.

Then, you are introduced to the Q.T. (Quality Training) Program, a *new* method of fast and effective sales training.

Next is a complete, professional sales presentation, using a week of *deeded vacation ownership* as the product. The *what, when, where, how and why* of *every* step of the sale from presale preparation to closing and follow up, is covered from A to Z.

The sales presentation is followed by a variety of sales related topics, including chapters on additional ways to overcome objections and close the sale.

For those selling any product other than vacation resort properties, particular attention should be paid to those techniques outlined in the chapter, "How to Customize the Sales Presentation to Your Product."

In addition, *How To* chapters are included on subjects such as building an effective management team and recruiting, hiring, and training the best sales force.

The last chapter offers "Words of Wisdom." Periodic review of this collection of sales adages will help you keep your sales and attitude on track.

Finally, there are test questions on the sales material covered to help you test and improve your retention level.

SUCCESS FORMULA

Learn well = **Earn** well = **Live** well

Introduction

Mary and John have received a letter of invitation to visit a nearby vacation resort. As an inducement, they will receive a complete set of luggage. They need only attend a brief, courteous tour and sales presentation.

They arrive at the resort with some cynicism and apprehension. Neighbors had visited a similar resort and told them stories of insensitive, high pressure sales tactics. This preconceived negative perception leads them to raise their defensive shield higher than normal. Mary and John make a pact not to purchase anything, no matter how good the offer sounds.

They are greeted by Tom, a friendly, disarming sales professional. About three hours and a hundred or more separate sales tactics later, Mary and John leave happy and excited about becoming the newest owners.

How could this drastic turn around happen in such a short span of time? Simply, Tom gave a *thoroughly professional sales presentation* designed specifically for people like Mary and John.

In today's complex vacation market, with a wide variety of vacation alternatives being offered to a more educated consumer, it is increasingly difficult to recruit, train, and elevate new sales people to Tom's level of expertise.

The author has been in resort sales and training for two decades. He knows the time and cost involved in bringing a rookie to pro status. If the training is not quick and effective, the cost can be staggering to the developer. Therefore, he is constantly searching for the better way.

To meet this challenge, the author knew he must depart from the conventional methods of the past. While practical and acceptable in their day, they are no longer cost effective.

Excessive training costs and high turnover of sales people diminish profits.

The author has devised a totally *new training method.* This *breakthrough* presents product information and sales techniques in a format more quickly absorbed by the trainee. Also, the job of reinforcing sound sales practices with the experienced sales line is made more efficient.

To fully appreciate the benefits of this new concept, hereinafter referred to as the **Q.T.** (for *Quality Training*) **Program,** one must first look at the problems inherent in conventional training.

Author's Note

The author has chosen to use the term "guests" when referring to prospective purchasers visiting a vacation resort. His reasons are two fold:

*First, most visitors to a resort who attend a sales presentation were **invited** by a sales or marketing representative of the developer. When you **invite** someone to visit, they become your **guest.** The dictionary definition of guest is a person **entertained** by another acting as **host.***

*Secondly, by referring to the prospective purchasers as guests, rather than in any other formal or derogatory manner, the salesperson is **constantly** reminded of the proper role the **host** must play.*

*Also, the author recognizes that in our modern business world, competent, professional women comprise an ever increasing percentage of most sales and management teams. Throughout this book, the male genders **he and his,** when not used to refer to a specific **male,** are intended to be **interchangeable** with the female genders **she** or **her.***

Knowing it would take many months to train the *novice* in *all* the sales tactics of the experienced professional, the average trainer settles for concentrating on product knowledge and a few basic points. The vast majority of training is then done on an ongoing basis, along with costly, on the job, trial and error fine tuning. *After* the rookie handles each prospect the trainer or manager critiques the rookie's performance. More often than not, it is a case of closing the barn door after the horse is out. The sale has been lost, but another valuable lesson is learned.

Each new bit of information is received by the rookie like a religious revelation. "*If* I had that sales tool last week, or that closing technique last month, I would have had a sale," he responds.

The dedicated trainer knows he is in a race against time. The goal is to impart enough know how into the trainee *before* he resigns in frustration and discouragement, or must be terminated for lack of production. When the race is lost, more than half the new recruits fail to make the grade. This never ending, costly cycle of recruiting and training is then repeated at frequent intervals.

The very root of the problem with conventional training methods is, in far too many cases, they take *too long* to impart sufficient knowledge for *acceptable* performance. Of course, a few highly motivated, success oriented persons with enthusiasm, charisma and a natural ability to relate well to people, do make the grade. It is difficult, however, to distinguish how much of *their* success was attributable to training as opposed to their own common sense and ambition.

The challenge confronting the experienced professional sales trainer is how to transfer the encyclopedia of knowledge he has stored in his memory bank to the rookie, within an *acceptable* time frame.

Using conventional training methods, the task is almost impossible. For each sales technique to be understood and properly executed, the trainer must clearly explain not only *what* to do, *when* and *where* to do it, but also *how* to do it.

To be sure the technique is permanently committed to memory, he must also show *why* it is appropriate.

The *what, when,* and *where,* or *mechanics,* of the sale are relatively a simple matter *to train.* Collectively, they are referred to as the "nuts and bolts" portion of the sales presentation.

The *how to,* or *methodology of the sale,* is more time consuming as it involves much repetition and role playing.

The *why,* or *psychology of the sale,* is by far the most time consuming and complex. Top trainers illustrate each point with sales stories. The stories help the trainee understand the psychology behind every action or response. The trainee who knows *why* he is following a certain strategy is more likely to commit the tactic permanently to memory than one who is just going through the motions like a robot.

Now that the problem has been clearly defined, let us now discuss the solution.

The *Q.T.* Program provides the solution; first, by recognizing the three basic parts to every sales technique consisting of the *mechanics (what, where, when),* the *methodology (how)* and the *psychology (why).* Rather than start by training all three parts on a *few* sales strategies, the *Q.T.* Program covers the *first* step, *mechanics,* from A to Z.

By telling a novice *what* he is expected to do from hello to goodbye, without *first* explaining the *how* and *why* of each step, the training process is greatly accelerated.

Some major advantages and benefits of establishing this new priority of order are as follows:

1) By providing the rookie with a comprehensive list, in proper sequence, of *all* the *mechanics (what, when,* and *where)* of a professional presentation, he is totally aware, from the *first* day of training, *exactly* what is expected of him and what tactics must be mastered for him to become proficient at his trade.

2) Although the rookie does not, in the beginning, know the *how* and *why* portion of each sales strategy, he at least knows the *right questions to ask;* "How do I control my prospects?" or "How do I go about establishing a common bond?" or "Why is it important to empathize with my guests?" or "Why is the first impression so important?" The more aggressive will ask more questions *sooner.*

3) The rookie can better rate his own progress by comparing the total list to how many of the tactics listed he can implement successfully.

4) Rookies sometimes become discouraged when they *think* they have learned all, or at least most, of what there is to know, and are still not yet successful. The list of mechanics shows them they still have a way to go.

5) As times change, the *Q.T.* Program can easily be updated. Simply delete any obsolete material and add the new material in its proper place.

6) To retain each person's own personality and individuality, the *Q.T.* Program uses *suggested ideas* and *outlines,* more than a prescribed "canned pitch." A *planned* presentation allows *each* salesperson to select words and phraseology that are natural and comfortable.

Now, let us start to become more professional than our competitors, on the *Q.T.*

Sales Lexicon

Advantage - A more favorable position; superiority.

Agreement - Being in harmony or accord. An understanding between two or more people.

A.I.D.S. - **Attention** - **Interest** - **Desire** = **Sale.**

Analogy - A comparison of similarities between two otherwise unlike things.

Assumptive - Taken for granted.

Attention - The act of keeping one's mind *closely* on something.

Attitude - A manner of acting, feeling or thinking that *shows* one's *disposition* or *opinion.*

Benefit - Anything contributing to an improvement in condition; advantage; help.

Catalyst - Person or thing acting as the stimulus in bringing about or hastening a result.

Chameleon - Lizard with ability to change color to blend with background.

Commitment - A pledge or promise to do something.

Common bond - Something in common that tends to unite.

Common Sense - Sound, practical judgment.

Communication - An *exchange* of ideas.

Compete - Endeavor to equal or surpass in achievement another person, usually one greatly admired.

Concern - Taken an interest.

Condition - Anything essential to the existence or occurrence of something else.

Control - Power to direct or regulate.

Conviction - The state or appearance of being *convinced.*

Creative - Having or showing imagination and inventiveness.

Credibility - The ability to have one's statements accepted as factual or one's professed motives accepted as the true ones.

Cynic - One who *denies* the *sincerity* of peoples' motives or actions.

Decision - The act of making up one's mind.

Desire - To wish or long for.

Diplomacy - Skill in dealing with people.

Discipline - Training that develops *self* control and efficiency.

Dissertation - A formal and lengthy discourse on some subject.

Dominant - Ruling, prevailing, or most influential person.

Emotion - Capability of having feelings aroused to a point of *awareness.*

Empathy - Ability to share in another's emotions and actions.

Enthusiasm - Intense or eager interest, zeal.

Equity - The value of property *beyond* the amount owed.

Exalted - Intensified or heightened action or effect.

Excuse - A pretended reason for conduct. Pretext.

Feature - A distinct or outstanding part, quality, or characteristic of something.

Finesse - The ability to handle *difficult* situations skillfully and diplomatically.

Goal - An object or end that one strives to attain.

Guest - A person *entertained* by another acting as host.

Inflation - *Sudden* drop in value of money and rise in prices.

Inflection - Any change in tone or pitch of the voice.

Intangible - That which cannot be touched — having no form or substance.

Intense - Having or showing strong emotion or purpose.

Interest - A feeling of intense concern or curiosity about something.

Justify - To show to be just, right, or in accord with reason.

K.I.S.S. - Keep it simple, stupid.

Knowledge - Awareness and understanding.

Leverage - Increased means of accomplishing some purpose.

Lexicon - A dictionary. The vocabulary of an individual or group.

Mechanical - Automatic, as if from force of habit, machine like, lacking spontaneity, expression, warmth.

Methodology - A system of methods. (*How?*)

Motivate - To provide with a motive; incite or impel.

Motive - Some *inner* drive that causes a person to do something or act in a certain way. Incentive. Goal.

Need - Required necessity.

Negative - Something denoting a quantity less than zero.

Objection - Reason for opposing, disapproving, disliking.

Optimist - One who expects the best outcome in any circumstance.

Orientation - Familiarization with and adaptation to a situation or environment.

Perseverance - Patient, continuing effort in spite of difficulty or obstacles.

Pessimist - One who expects the worst outcome in any circumstance.

Positive - Having the mind set - confident - assured.

Prejudge - To judge beforehand without the benefit of all the facts.

Pressure - To make demands requiring immediate attention.

Pretext - A false reason or motive put forth to hide the real one.

Professional - A person who does something with *great skill.*

Prospect - A likely or *prospective* customer.

Psychology - The science dealing with the mental and emotional processes of the mind. (*Why?*)

Qualify - To be or become qualified by meeting certain requirements.

Quality - The degree of *excellence* or *superiority* which anything possesses.

Question - Something asked to *learn* or test another's knowledge.

Reason - Explanation or justification.

Recognition - Acknowledgment, approval, gratitude.

Relate - To show understanding and awareness in a personal relationship.

Sell - To establish faith, confidence or belief in *oneself.*

Solution - The answer to a problem.

Spontaneity - Produced or done *naturally.*

Subtle - Keen, expert, skillful, crafty.

Suppose - To *assume* to be true to illustrate a proof.

Sympathy - Pity or compassion as felt for another's troubles.

Tact - Delicate perception of the right thing to say or do *without offending.*

Tangible - That which can be touched; having form or substance.

Trust - Firm belief or confidence in the honesty, integrity, reliability of another person; faith.

Urgency - Need for action.

Use - The enjoyment of property; to bring into action.

Vacation - Freedom from any activity, or time for recreation.

Value - The degree of *usefulness, importance, desirability* which a thing is *thought of* as being worth; *fair price* or *return.*

Versatile - Competent in many things; adaptable.

Want - Desire, craving, longing, wish for.

Warm (up) - Genial, cordial, sincere, friendly; "close to discovering something;" "getting warm."

Zeal - Enthusiasm; fanaticism.

CHAPTER ONE

Presale Preparation

Part I
The Mechanics of Presale Preparation

Get enough **sleep.**

Eat breakfast.

Do some **exercise.**

Dress for success.

Listen to motivational tapes enroute to work.

Get in a positive, upbeat frame of **mind.**

Keep vehicle in top condition.

Leave personal problems behind.

Update inventory, check the bulletin board, organize your sales materials **before the sales meeting.**

Avoid negative people.

Mentally visualize first sale.

Set short and long term goals.

Devise ways and means of improving your personal and professional qualities.

Part II
The Methodology and Psychology
of Presale Preparation

1. When questioned about his genius, Thomas Edison replied,

"Genius is 1% inspiration and 99% perspiration."

For Thomas Edison, four hours sleep each night was sufficient. The average person requires between six and eight hours of sleep to perform at maximum efficiency. Plan late night social functions for days off. The sales game requires you to **think,** not **doze,** on your feet.

"You can't hoot with the owls and still fly with the eagles."

2. Eating breakfast, including fruit juice, provides the energy needed to perform at your best for the **entire** day. Low blood sugar levels cause some loss of concentration and increase errors, particularly when working with figures. Fruit juices maintain blood sugar levels throughout the day.

"Work smart, not hard."

3. Keeping in good physical condition will improve your overall sense of well being, and keep sick days to a minimum. A healthy body is the foundation for a keen mind.

4. To **be** successful, you must **look successful. Dress** compatible with Company dress code and the resort atmosphere. Whether formal or casual dress, neatness and cleanliness are always a **must.** Some guests are turned off by an unkempt appearance. Sales is a numbers game. The well groomed salesperson assures the numbers are in his favor.

Whatever the dress code, there are certain basic guidelines to follow:

A. Colors can affect the mood of your guests. White denotes purity, blue sincerity. Green or pastel colors are relaxing. Red signifies anger.

B. Exceptionally loud or "trendy" clothes are offensive to some. Herringbone or bold patterns are **optically** distracting.

C. Colors may be bright, but color combinations should always be coordinated. Mismatched clothing projects the image of a disorganized person.

D. Quality, well tailored clothes are visual evidence of success.

5. **Upbeat music** or **motivational tapes** create the proper frame of mind. They can also prevent you from dwelling on any personal problems that could detract from your best performance.

6. Although good **preventive maintenance** will not **guarantee** any vehicle will be reliable 100% of the time, it will put the odds heavily in your favor.

7. Arrive at work early enough to do everything that should be done **before** you greet your first guest. **"We don't plan to fail, we fail to plan."**

8. Every resort has its share of **negative people.** These pessimists, to avoid the label of pessimist, call themselves **realists.** The best way to maintain a positive attitude is by **avoiding** these forecasters of doom.

9.   The sale should start by visualizing it in your mind, long before meeting a guest. Then you automatically convey a positive attitude to that guest.

"What the mind can conceive, we can achieve."

10.   There is no way to tell how far we have come, unless a destination has been set. **Short** and **long term goals,** both personal and professional, provide a yardstick for measuring success. A larger sense of purpose can help weather the ups and downs that are part of the sales profession. Set realistic, attainable goals, otherwise they create frustration and disappointment. As each level of your goals are met, they should be raised slightly, constantly providing an achievable challenge.

11.   Be objective, but not overly critical, in analyzing your own personal and professional qualities. **Before** blaming the Company, the management, your peers or the guests for a sales slump, ask yourself **honestly** if you in any way **contributed** to the problem. Chance are, there are some areas **you** might improve. Make the necessary improvements and move forward, but never **dwell** on past mistakes.

CHAPTER TWO

The Greeting, Warm Up and Product Presentation

Part I
Mechanics of The Greeting, Warm Up and Product Presentation

Give friendly greeting to **all** guests.

Make a positive first impression on them.

***Keep** good eye contact with them.

***Be enthusiastic,** exciting, convincing and colorful.

Request guests follow to the sales area.

Seat them properly.

Maintain control **throughout.**

Help guests relax and be comfortable.

***Use** humor to relax them.

Overcome their initial apprehension and synicism.

Prove you have good intentions.

Anticipate and **Answer** common questions guests have upon arrival.

Inform them when and where they will receive any promised incentives.

Lower tention by telling them exactly what they will be doing today.

** To be used **throughout total** presentation.*

Get their attention and interest.

Break pact as often as necessary.

Depressurize guests by acknowledging they have no obligation to purchase.

Build credibility of company.

Justify and explain marketing program.

Justify the first day offer.

Minimize significance of (premium) incentives as compared to opportunity offered today.

*Assume the posture of a knowledgable, concerned, professional **advisor.**

Establish your competency.

Refer to members from their home area.

Mention any well known and highly respected persons who already have joined the program. Use testimonials.

Seek a common bond with them.

Share information about yourself.

Exhibit pictures of your family to family oriented guests.

Build trust and rapport.

Make sincere compliments about their clothing, jewelry, personal appearance or attitude.

Qualify, rather than prejudge them.

To be used **throughout total presentation.*

Verbally ignore minor negative comments of guests, but acknowledge them with body language.

Determine their past vacation lifestyle and future vacation preferences.

Find out what they liked or disliked about past vacations.

Find out which one in the party is the dominant person.

Admire their work skills.

*****Be empathetic** to their problems, needs and objectives.

*****Hear** what they **mean,** rather than just what they say.

*****Listen** responsively and selectively.

*****Respond to** questions quickly, then qualify answers, if necessary.

*****Use** positive motivational words and phrases.

*****Avoid** negative words.

*****Respond** to a question with a question — when unsure of the purpose and motive of their question.

*****Preserve** 100% credibility throughout.

*****Observe** their body language.

Adjust the rate and **method** of presentation to blend with their personality types.

Give guests **"mental pauses."**

Be flexible and versatile.

*****To be used **throughout total** presentation.*

Make presentation a non-competitive win/win situation.

Orient them as to resort location in relation to nearest major towns and local area attractions.

Familiarize guests as to location of amenities and product in relation to the sales office.

Deliver brief verbal map tour. **Paint** mental pictures.

*__Use__ graphics (to enforce important points).

*__Make__ all written material large and legible.

Show the problems associated with other forms of vacations.

Clearly explain the mechanics of the program.

Demonstrate program solutions, savings and benefits.

Explain flexibility and purpose of the exchange program.

Show other benefits associated with the exchange program.

Keep the dream within their reach.

Show film, video tape, visual aids.

Ask more questions. **Request** they expand on answers.

Promise only what can be delivered.

Know all you tell — don't tell all you know.

Prepare guests for tour.

*_To be used_ **_throughout total_** _presentation._

Part II
The Methodology and Psychology of The Greeting, Warm Up and Product Presentation

Give a **warm smile** and a **firm handshake** to your guests and **all** in their party.

Greeting **all** in your guests' party is a matter of **common courtesy** and secondly, any person or persons you ignore or alienate might be party to, or have influence upon, the buying decision.

You only have **one** opportunity to make a good **first impression.** By starting off on the right foot, you can earn the friendship and trust of your guests more **quickly.**

Keep good **eye contact** by looking your guests "square in the eye" when greeting and throughout your presentation. This is especially true when you are making important statements or claims your guests **must believe.**

People **mistrust** those who do not maintain good eye contact. The person with poor eye contact is construed to be **untrustworthy** and **evasive.** The salesperson can also assess the **sincerity** and **honesty** of his guests by observing the degree of eye contact his guests maintain with **him.** This is particulary important to note when the guest is responding to significant questions requiring commitment or honesty.

Dark glasses, unless in bright sunlight, or required by prescription, should **never** be worn during a sales presentation.

Be enthusiastic about the **company** you represent, the **product** being offered, and the **opportunity** you have to **help** your guests achieve their vacation goals and objectives.

Enthusiasm takes several forms. For the extroverted salesperson, it may involve a great deal of hand motions and other body language.

For the introvert, sincerity and conviction in the presentation can convey the enthusiasm **that** salesperson has for his product.

Whatever the social style of the salesperson, the presentation **must be exciting** and **colorful.** Enthusiasm is contagious. The guests very seldom, if ever, become excited about a program that is presented in a dull and bland manner. Vacations are **fun.** Be sure your presentation sets the proper mood.

Request your guests follow you from the reception area to the sales area. The sales presentation should **not** begin until your guests are properly seated.

Your guests should be **seated together,** close to the table, **opposite** the salesperson. With this seating arrangement, it is easy to maintain eye contact and simultaneously observe the body language of more than one person.

Maintaining control throughout your presentation starts with the greeting. "Please follow me" and "Would you sit here, John, and, Mary, sit next to John."are the first, subtle measures of control. Few sales are made where the salesperson loses control of his guests.

When the salesperson allows his guests to ignore or show little response to his presentation, contact is quickly lost. This is especially true when the salesperson poses a question to his guests and receives merely a grunt or no response at all. This situation can be remedied by **repeating** any question that is not answered fully or satisfactorily. This can be done **tactfully** by acting as though the guest had either misunderstood or did not hear the question posed the first time.

Another method of maintaining control throughout is the **book story.** Often guests will deluge the salesperson with questions on subjects to be covered at some later time in the presentation. Answering too many questions, prematurely and out of context, can take the total presentation off on some confusing and unproductive tangents. At the first sign of this problem, the salesperson can maintain control with the following story.

"Mary and John, each resort has its own story. Each part of the story is like a chapter in a book. My job is to present the total story to you, chapter by chapter. Now, if we were to read Chapter I and then skip to Chapter XII, then backtrack to Chapter II, then jumped to Chapter VIII, you would eventually receive the whole story, but not in a way that it would be easy to digest. That makes sense, doesn't it?"

When your guests **confirm** your logic, continue: "It is my intention to go through the **whole** story, chapter by chapter. Please feel free to interrupt me with any questions you might have relative to the chapter we are discussing at the moment. When we finish the last chapter, virtually everything of importance about our resort will have been disclosed to you. At that time, I'll answer any other questions you may have, or, if I cannot give you a complete answer, I will call in my sales manager for assistance."

"Don't you agree this will give you **all the** information in a clearer, more concise manner?"

Upon agreement, you can proceed with your presentation. Anytime in the presentation your guests ask a question **that is irrelevant or premature,** you need only respond, with a smile, "That's Chapter VII, John," or "That's Chapter VI, Mary." Your guests will acknowledge and you will **maintain control.**

Help your guests to relax and be comfortable. Most people are apprehensive in strange surroundings, especially in a sales situation. A broad smile and a humorous remark are a good way to "break the ice."

Unless your guests are a referral of an existing owner, they view the resort sales presentation with some degree of cynicism. Until a measure of trust is established, the cynic is not receptive to any presentation.

The best way to break down defensive barriers quickly is to answer the common questions guests have on their mind upon arrival:

"How long is this going to take?"

"When will I receive my promised incentives?"

"What is expected of us?"

"Who are you?"

"Who is the Company behind this offer?"

"What are your intentions?"

"Does anyone ever win a major prize (sweepstakes only)?"

(Intent Statement) You can lower tension levels by telling your guests exactly what you will be doing today.

"First, I'll tell you about my company, our methods of marketing and something about myself."

"Then I'll ask you to share some information about yourselves. This information will help me customize our program to your vacation lifestyle and budget, should our program solve any of your vacation problems or help you reach your vacation goals and objectives."

'Next, I'll show you the features and benefits of our product, and the ways you can save time and money, while enjoying more luxurious vacations. How does that sound to you, Mary and John?"

Once we have agreement and the **attention** and **interest** of our guests, we can proceed.

The next item on the agenda will be the **fun** part. The actual tour of our resort. "I'll show you our vacation units, as well as the many amenities that will be yours to enjoy should you elect to join our family."

"After the tour, I will **summarize** all the features and benefits of our resort. Then, I will explain **additional** benefits you will receive because of our affiliation with a world wide vacation exchange program.

"Finally, I'll show you how affordable it is to become our newest members.

"Of course, you have absolutely no obligation to purchase. I only ask that you keep an open mind. Fair enough?"

"If you **like** what you see and hear today, if you see the **value,** and it's **affordable,** I'm going to ask you to become our newest members." (Breaking Pact)

(Depressurize) "However, if you **don't** like it, don't see the **value,** or it's not **affordable,** then I'll shake your hand, get your gifts and we will part friends. Is that okay with you?"

Get agreement and a **handshake from all in party.**

Now that we have lowered the tension level, it is time to build credibility, trust and rapport.

Building Credibility

A.   Give past history of Company. Explain financial strength of Company, commitments to our owners, and future growth potential.

B.   **Justify** and explain marketing methods. **Minimize** the significance of incentives (gifts) as compared to the opportunity offered today. Relate first day offer to retail stores one day only sales. (A **cost effective** means of marketing that saves money for the purchaser and developer alike.) The marketer must, and does, deliver on all promises.

C.   Assume the posture of a knowledgable, concerned, professional **advisor.** Let your guests know of your professional qualifications, as well as long term commitment to serve your owners.

D.   Refer to other members from guests' home town.

E.   Mention any well known and highly respected persons who already have joined your program. Use written testimonials to document.

Building trust and rapport

One of the best methods of building rapport with your guests is to establish a **common bond** with them. Did you live in the same area at any time? Do you have any common acquaintances? Do you belong to any of the same social or fraternal orders? Have you worked at the same occupation or served in the same branch of the service? Politics and religion can also be the basis for a common bond, but these subjects should be avoided unless there is a high degree of certainty that you share the same opinions.

Literally every person you speak with at length has **some** basis for a common bond with the salesperson. For family orientated guests, showing pictures of **your** family could **instill** the needed confidence that you are a stable and responsible individual.

Sincere compliments about a particularly attractive item of clothing or jewelry the guest is wearing, or a **genuine** compliment about your guests intelligence or positive attitude will help bring down defenses.

Now that we have shared a good deal of information about our Company and ourselves, our guests will psychologically be more willing to share with us information about themselves.

We can obtain the necessary information from our guest in a number of ways. Either we can simply ask pertinent questions, taking notes on any significant and useful data, or we can employ a preprinted guest survey form. The form can be completed by guests and then **reviewed** by the salesperson, or the salesperson can fill out the survey, after justifying to his guests the information is to **help** customize the program to the guests' specific needs. Whichever method is used, the salesperson should always ask questions in a low key, friendly, interested manner. **Never** should the survey process resemble an **interrogation.**

The **survey** is meant to help you **qualify** your guests for the program, not **prejudge** them. Any negative responses should be ignored verbally, but acknowledged with body language. Positive responses should be reinforced by the salesperson.

The **primary purpose** of the guest survey is to determine the guests past vacation lifestyle and future vacation plans. Also, their occupation and number of dependents can help determine their affordability range.

A few key questions will go a long way towards determining your guests likes and dislikes.

"Where did you go on your last vacation?"

"What did you like best about it?"

"What did you like least about it?"

"If you could take a dream vacation, where time and money were no object whatsoever, where would you go?"

Be sure to pose **every** question to **each** guest. Their answers may be surprisingly different — The husband likes a sandy beach, but the wife prefers the mountains. Usually **one** of the spouses is more outspoken and dominant. Be sure the dominant personality is on your side.

Of all the questions on the typical guest survey, the one that many sales people fail to capitalize upon is the **occupations** of the guests.

More than money, most people yearn for **recognition.** So give them the recognition they so richly deserve.

The laborer can be admired for his industriousness.

The skilled mechanic praised for his dexterity.

The white collar worker, be they teacher, engineer, scientist, computer programmer or any other field requiring extensive study, can be complimented for their dedication and intelligence.

The musician ackowledged for his talent.

The doctor, lawyer or any other self-employed professional admired for their success and independence.

Civil service and social workers can be admired for their contributions to to public welfare.

By showing appreciation and admirtation for their skills, and talents, including the housewife and other, who may have the most difficult task of all, your guests will perceive you to be a sensitive, concerned person.

An easy way to show empathy is to make a mental list of the **gripes** of every profession. Then make your guests aware that **you are aware** of their daily frustrations. Following are some examples of how empathy can be used as a sales tool:

"Mary, being a **nurse** certainly must put you under a lot of pressure. Life and death decisions have to be made on a daily basis. You surely need a break from the long hours and stress of your job. **You do all the work and the doctor gets all the credit.** It takes a very special type of person to do your job."

"John, as a police officer, your job has to be one of the most demanding and frustrating in today's society. You risk your life, work long hours on different shifts and **do not get** half the **respect** and **support** from the public that **you deserve.** You get a little rough with a criminal, and you are accused of police brutality. When you succeed in arresting a criminal, he walks away free on some technicality of the law. Let me tell you this, John, I'm one citizen who really **appreciates** what you do out there."

If your comments are sincere, not patronizing, your guests could **already be sold** at this point. Why? Because we **want** to buy from people we like, and we tend to like people who understand us.

Being empathetic to the problems, needs and objectives is often more important to the sale than the product itself.

Asking all the questions in this book will prove of little value to those who have not learned to **listen.**

Most people are guilty of "lazy listening." They only hone in on the last few words of each sentence in order to get the gist of what is being said.

The true sales professional learns to **listen intently, selectively,** and **responsively.** He listens to **each** word and any changes in voice inflection that provide clues to what the guests **mean,** rather than just what they **said.**

A person who states "I want to look at your resort," differs from another who states "I **just** want to look at your resort." The first person made a simple, unqualified statement. The second person, by inserting the word **just,** qualified his statement to mean "I don't wish to purchase, I **just** want to look." Both can be sold, but your approach to the second, more defensive person, would be slightly different.

One guest states your program "is fantastic," the other guest says "it **sounds** (or **seems**) great." Which one might have some reservations? The second guest, by inserting the words **"sounds** or **seems"** may need additional reassurance.

The professional also listens to the **inflection** in his guests' voice. A change of emphasis from one word to another in a sentence can **change the entire meaning.**

Let us take the statement, "I will not give you the money." If the emphasis was on the word **I**, it would imply **someone else** may give you the money. Shift the emphasis to the word **you**, it implies that I may give the money to **another party.** Shift the emphasis to the word **money.** The same statement now implies the giver may **substitute** something else **for the money.**

USING EXCITING, POSITIVE WORDS

A.   **Vary** your voice tone and inflections. A monotone can make the most exciting programs seem boring.

B.   **Use positive** words that **reinforce** your product and **avoid negative** words that cause doubt and fear.

Positive words that instill confidence include proven, health, you, guests' names, save money, fun, vital, safety, security, new, love, results, right, positive, advantage, trust, deserve, happy, comfort, truth.

An **offer** is better than a **deal.**

Own or **try** is better than **buy.**

Invest is better than **pay.**

Choice is better than **decision.**

Easy is better than **hard.**

Value is better than **cost.**

To confirm whether you have succeeded in communicating a given point to your guests, it is far better to say "Have I made myself clear on this" than to say, "Do you understand?" The first statement implies the **responsibility** to convey information lies with the salesperson. The second statement could be construed by your guests as questioning their mentality or ability to comprehend.

At the end of a successful sales presentation, the buyer is not reluctant to **"O.K. this agreement,"** but could be apprehensive about "signing this contract." Most people are preconditioned to seek legal advice before signing **contracts.**

C.   When your guests ask a question, you can **clarify** the purpose and motive of the question by answering with another question.

Example:

Question: "Do you allow **campers** on this property?"

Response: "Do you **own** or **plan to buy** a camper?"

The response will tell you in which direction to proceed.

D.   When answering questions, **respond quickly,** then **qualify** your answer, if necessary. Long delays in responding to questions will lead your guests to believe you are **inventing** answers, rather than being a knowledgable professional who **has** the answers.

Example:

Question: "Do we have to pay any kind of maintenance fees?"

Response: "Yes you do. **However,** the first year is free as part of your first day benefits."

Before beginning your product presentation, you must fully understand the critical importance of maintaining **100% credibility.**

If **99%** of your presentation is factual and believable, the **1%** that is not totally believable can cost a sale.

The sale can be lost in two ways. First, if the doubt created in the mind of your guest by the 1% of the presentation that was **not** believable is strong enough, your guests will lack the confidence to make a buying commitment. Secondly, even if your overall presentation was enthusiastic and dynamic enough to induce your guests to buy more on emotion than logic ("under the ether"), the one untruthful or exaggerated statement will **stay** with the buyers after the close.

It is only a matter of time until the seed of doubt takes root and the buyers inevitably ask themselves, "If he was not being totally honest about one thing, how can I be sure everything **else** was the truth?" The doubt feeds upon itself until anxiety and uncertainty cause the buyer to cancel his purchase. Don't give doubt any place to take root. Be **100% credible** at all times.

A good presentation requires good **communication.** The definition of communication is: an **exchange** of information. While you dispense information about your product, you must also be **gathering** information about your guests. Their verbal responses alone are but a small part of the total picture.

Tone of voice and **body language** are far more revealing than the words alone. The words are merely a reflection of the outward **behavior.** The tone and inflection of the voice give us clues to **feelings.** The body language telegraphs the **thinking** of guests.

To the professional salesperson the **furrowed brow** of the guests sends a message that his guests **do not** clearly **understand** the topic. He then covers the same point more clearly and slowly.

Eyes rolled up indicate **doubt.** That point should be covered in a more credible way.

Arms folded, the guest is **defensive.** Work on lowering the resistance level.

Feet placed squarely on the floor, face cupped in hand, leaning in a forward position means you have their attention and interest. **(A. I. D. S.)** represents the steps to the sale. **Attention — Interest — Desire — Sale.**

To be sure **every** guest understands the total presentation, we must adjust the **rate** of our presentation to suit the capacity of each guest to absorb information.

A simple way to remember this point is to solve this problem:

Assuming we turned a water faucet on **full blast,** which would fill **first,** a one-ounce **shot glass** or a wide mouthed **gallon jug?**

The answer, of course, is the gallon jug. It has the **capacity** to accept the water. With the shot glass, the water would splash out as quickly as it went in. The vessel is **too small** to absorb the water coming out **full blast.**

Some of the guests are shot glasses. Others are gallon jugs or something in between. **Adjust your spout** to suit your guests.

To make a buying commitment, your guests must have **some** time to **absorb and consider** the information and offer you have made. A non-stop verbal barrage from hello to goodbye creates several major problems:

A.   The guests feel **pressured.**

B.   The **attention span** of most people ranges between 5 to 15 minutes. Once that period is exceeded, the mind tends to drift or shut out further information as a protective measure. This is similar in nature to the "pain threshold" athletes experience when they have pushed their bodies to the limits of their **physical** capabilities.

If time is not allowed **during** the presentation for your guests to absorb the information and consider the offer, most will want additional time **at home** "to think about it." Any chance for a **same day** sale is lost.

Rather than a non-stop presentation, your guests should be given "**mental pauses**" at regular intervals. The guests will feel they are **not** being pressured and will have ample opportunity to understand and act on your offer.

The **social style** of your guests will also determine the type of presentation that should be made.

The hard driving executive may seek **control.** He is most likely to purchase from a competent professional who lays out the facts and gets quickly to the **bottom line.**

The engineer or accountant may prefer a slower, more **logical, factual** presentation. They also would be impressed by competency. **Analytical** types are almost obsessed with a need to be **right.**

The **expressive, outgoing extrovert** is more apt to purchase from someone he likes based upon an entertaining presentation that appeals more to his **emotions** than simply logic.

The laid back, easy going **agreeable type** will also be more vulnerable to a **slow, emotional** presentation that offers assurances and guarantees.

The professional salesperson must be flexible and versatile. He must be natural and yet assume a personality that blends harmoniously with that of his guests, much like the chameleon, a lizard that changes colors to blend with its background.

One of the most important points we can convey to our guests is that the sales offer is strictly a win/win situation. You are there to **help** your guests **solve** any vacation problems, satisfy their needs and **assist** them to achieve their objectives and goals. We do not **compete** with our guests, because with any competition there is a winner and a loser. Convince your guests that **everyone wins** when they join your resort. When they pass up your outstanding offer, you **both lose.**

A good place to begin your product presentation is with a **map orientation.** Show the location of your resort in relation to the **closest major cities** or towns and local **area attractions.** Also, with a map of your resort, you can familiarize your guests with the location of the amenities and product within the resort. Use a pointer to show the route to be followed in touring the resort. If not a driving tour, floor plans and color photos can serve the same purpose.

The Product Presentation

Graphics and **published articles** from unbiased, respected, outside sources will often reinforce your credibility on important points of your presentation.

Any written portion of the presentation should be written large and legibly. The figures you wish to **stress** should be apart and in **larger print** than any other written material on the same page.

The **continuity** of a sales presentation is as important, if not more so, than the **content.** An endless array of facts and figures, not introduced in proper sequence, can be confusing and counterproductive.

Keep in mind that sales is basically a problem solving process. By first identifying the current or future vacation problems of your guests, you can then offer solutions.

You can start with very general problems and work your way through several problems and solution cycles until all the solutions, savings, advantages and benefits have been explained.

Example:

The product is a **deeded** week of vacation **timesharing** at a resort that features fully furnished 2 bedroom units, complete with fully equipped kitchens.

Mary and John have been staying in resort hotels for their past few vacations. They also considered purchasing a vacation condominium. The salesperson must clearly explain his product and show how it is superior to other vacation alternatives.

First, we discuss the **problems** of **hotel/motel** vacationing:

A. **Expensive**—money is **spent**; not recoverable; no deed; no equity.

B. **Reservation** hassles—may not be available when you need it.

C. **Costs** subject to inflationary increases each year.

D. **Dining out** is expensive, especially for large families.

E. **Accommodations** are small and offer little privacy.

An **advantage** to this type of vacation is the **variety of locations** from which one can choose.

Now, let's list the major **problems** associated with purchasing a **vacation condominium.**

A. **Purchase prices** in resort areas are **prohibitive** for the vast majority of Americans.

B. **Pay** 52 weeks a year for only a few weeks' use.

C. **Maintenance,** insurance, utilities, taxes, furnishings, landscaping, are additional year round expenses.

D. The vacation condominium is in a **fixed location;** no variety of locations.

The primary **advantage** of the whole ownership condominium is that the owner who **can** afford the purchase price and maintenance will gradually **build equity.** The mortgage payments reduce the outstanding mortgage balance while inflation may increase the resale value as well.

The Solution

1. First show origin, history and mechanics of timesharing.

2. Show how **deeded** vacation ownership offers **both** an opportunity to **build equity** and **variety of locations** through affiliation with a national or international exchange service. The **best** of both worlds at a **fraction** of the cost!

The Exchange Program

When your resort is affiliated with a world wide exchange program, it is relatively easy to build the dream. By painting mental pictures, your guests can visualize themselves laying on a sandy beach in the Bahamas, or sipping a pina colada at poolside in Hawaii. They can envision the fun and excitement of a whirlwind tour of the historical cities of Europe. Less exotic, but more practical for many, is the opportunity to exchange to resorts within driving distance of the home resort.

Most exchange services offer fringe benefits such as discounted air fares and car rentals. While they are seldom the **sole** reason your guests will purchase, they do **enhance** the perceived value of the total package.

A word of caution when selling the dream vacation—keep the dream **within their reach.**

For the very **affluent,** we can sell the **world.**

For the middle and upper middle class, it is best to **feature** the United States, neighboring countries, and the **closest tropical islands.**

For the marginal income family, especially those with several children, it is best to concentrate on resorts within a reasonable driving distance.

The major **reason** for keeping the dream within the reach of your guests is that the emotion and excitement generated during the sales presentation seldom outlasts the **legal rescission period** during which your guests may cancel the sales contract.

Why would the **marginal** buyer cancel his dream vacation to **Hawaii?** Quite simply, after the emotions of the moment wore off, our guests reentered the **real** world. The round trip **airfare** for a family of four, from New York to Hawaii, was more than they could possibly budget for their annual vacations. With great reluctance and disappointment, they cancel their timeshare purchase.

A few months later, the same family receives another invitation to a different timeshare resort. This time the salesperson **stresses** resorts within easy driving distance, keeping the dream within their reach. He does **mention** Hawaii and other exotic destinations, but reserves those vacations for special, once in a lifetime, vacations. The second honeymoon, the special anniversary, or when some major financial obligation, such as the home mortgage, has been satisfied. This keeps the long range dream alive, and the current vacations **affordable.**

Most exchange services provide film or video tapes showing people like your guests enjoying vacations in a variety of locations. The moderator is usually a celebrity type who enjoys a high level of recognition and credibility. These **visual aids** are of **immense value** to the salesperson in building **desire** for his product. Precisely **where** the visual aids should be inserted in the sales presentation is a matter of judgment and preference of the individual sales manager and/or developer.

Resorts in the most popular tourist areas, where **demand** for accommodations often **exceeds** the **supply,** are known as **destination resorts.** These resorts may have nationwide or even international appeal. Those resorts that are less well known and appeal primarily to persons living in the same region of the country are referred to as **home resorts.**

The mechanics of most vacation exchange systems are such that the resorts that are **most in demand** also receive **some priority** in **exchanging** for other resorts. Whether or not the salesperson should **stress** this point depends upon which side of the fence his resort is located.

During the product presentation, the experienced sales professional does at least as much **asking** as he does **telling.** He also has his guests expand on their answers. Most guests will provide all the information you need, **provided** the questions are asked in such a manner that convey **genuine** interest and concern. Ask like a **warm friend**, not a **cold interrogator.**

When answering questions as to what your program can do for your guests, do not make any promises that cannot be delivered. By exaggerating the benefits, you could create a "too good to be true" syndrome. Your program **can** have some **limitations** and still be the best way to go. **Admitting** some **limitations** to your program is often the very thing that prompts the educated consumer to purchase.

Each resort will have its own code of ethics to which the salesperson **must** adhere. Also, the salesperson must let his conscience and common sense be his guide. "Know all you tell, but don't tell all you know" is sound advice. **Feature** the strengths of your program, more than the **weaknesses** of your competitors.

Now, with a **tantalizer statement** such as — "If you have no further questions, Mary and John, we are ready for your personally guided tour of the best vacation program to be offered to the public in your lifetime." On to the tour!

CHAPTER THREE

The Tour
Part I
Mechanics of The Tour

Furnish guests a map to follow along.

Sell what it **does,** rather than what it **is.**

Explain features, benefits and advantages of product. **(Hope of gain)**

Highlight areas your resort compares favorably to competitors.

Stress features and benefits that are of **particular interest** to guests, **mention** the **others.**

Stay physically and mentally **close** to guests.

Shift your presentation **gradually** from **third person** to **second person.**

Execute "takeaways", if needed. **(Fear of loss)**

Use tie down.

Ask active, involvement questions.

Utilize trial closes.

Reevaluate affordability range of guests.

Define product selection to be offered to them.

Make sure benefits outweigh any concerns.

Utilize third party stories.

Build value.

Create want, need, desire.

Part II
The Methodology and Psychology

As quickly as possible you should make:

Your guests feel **comfortable** and **orientated.** This can be accomplished easily with a full color wall map of the **tour route.** This "fun" map should be bordered with a montage of renderings or photos of the amenities and facilities of the resort. Give **each** guest a small laminated map with which to follow along.

If not a car tour, use renderings and floor plans.

As you show the features of your resort, tell what each feature can **do** for your guests, rather than just explain what it **is.**

For every feature, there is a **benefit.** Many features have **advantages** not offered by competitors. If your guests do not avail themselves of your outstanding offer, they often are faced with undesirable **alternatives.**

Example # 1:

Feature: **Heated** Indoor Pool

Benefits: Fun, healthy

Advantage: **Year round** swimming

Alternatives: **Shovel Snow** while our owners frolic in the pool

Example # 2:

Feature: Luxurious 2 Bedroom Vacation Unit

Benefits: Comfort and convenience (kitchen)

Advantages: More private and liveable than average hotel room

Alternatives: Reservation hassles, high food costs, and constant inflationary increases in hotel rates.

When showing your resort, **highlight** those areas of your resort that are superior to your competitors.

Show **all** the features of your resort. **Stress** those features that are of particular interest to your guests, and simply **mention** the others. No one likes to pay for facilities they do not intend to use.

To the golfer, you show a **golf resort** that happens to also have tennis courts.

To the tennis player, you show a **tennis resort** that happens to have a golf course.

Stay physically close to your guests throughout the presentation. You cannot **monitor body language** from a distance. Also, by staying close, you can **control** and participate in conversation.

Sales pressure applied **before** need, want, desire and value have been established **alienates** your guests and builds buyer resistance. Proper timing and finesse can get your guests deeply involved, if you **help them** to **gradually** become a part of the program. Start out using **third party stories.** When your guests are relaxed, interested and involved, shift to **second party** mode.

Example:

Start off with **"Our owners enjoy"**

Then — **"If** you become an owner"

Then — **"When** you become an owner"

Finally — **"You — Yours"**

All of selling can be broken down into two major parts.

1. **Hope of gain** — all the benefits you will derive by purchasing the product.

2. **Fear of loss** — the negative things that will happen if the prospect does not take advantage of the offer **now.**

Let us for a moment stray from resort sales to illustrate how the same basic **sale principles** are applied in auto sales.

Example:

Product — Luxurious, expensive, new, fire engine red, high performance, convertible Sports Car

Hope of Gain (Benefits)

A. Prestige

B. Outstanding acceleration

C. Excellent road handling

D. Resale value

E. Quality material and workmanship

F. Means to publicly express your personality

G. (Subtle) Appealing to opposite sex

Fear of Loss (Takeaway)

A. Last one in stock

B. Possible price increase

E. Low financing rate ends

F. Have other buyers interested

C. Last one this
color

G. Today **only** offer

D. Sale ends

When making your presentation you can keep guests **involved** with the use of **"tie downs."**

Finish statements with, isn't it? doesn't it? wouldn't you? The tie down **requires an answer** from your guests. By evoking some response, you are assured your guests are fully aware of every point you wish to make. The tie down will also help you **gain agreement** and **commitment.** This can be useful when the time comes to **close the sale.**

Example:

A. "This is a beautiful pool, **isn't it,** Mary?"

B. "This unit would accommodate your whole family comfortably, **wouldn't it,** John?"

C. "This entire program makes a lot of sense, **doesn't it,** John and Mary?"

Use **active** questions that require guests to answer based upon the **assumption** they will be our newest members.

Examples:

A. "In which bedroom would the kids be sleeping?"

B. "Would you be using the unit **primarily** to vacation here, or for exchanging to other locations?"

Use **trial closes** to "take the temperature" of your guests. The **feedback** will let you know how **close** you are to having a commitment.

Example:

A. "This certainly looks like something you and your family would benefit from for many years, **don't you agree?"**

B. "The best time for you to start enjoying more luxurious vacations **and** saving money is **now,** isn't it, John and Mary?"

C. "The two bedroom unit is well within your price range and budget, **wouldn't you say?"**

When you review the guest survey, you know the occupation and approximate gross income of your guests. The average American family may have 5% to 10% of their gross income that is **not** committed to current obligations. This disposable or discretionary annual income can be broken down to a monthly amount. By comparing **that** amount with the monthly payments required to purchase your product, you can **begin** to qualify your guests financially.

Disposable income calculations are merely a **guideline,** subject to many variables. Your guests may have substantial savings or equity in insurance policies and real estate that could be quickly converted to cash. On the other hand, they may be overextended due to recent large purchases.

The more information the salesperson can **extract with finesse,** the sooner he can zero in on the **specific** type product that would be in the affordability range of his guests.

Once you have determined which price level is affordable for your guests, your presentation should be adjusted accordingly.

From this point in the presentation, the salesperson must **stress** the benefits of the **affordable** product. It would not make sense to discuss all the features of a full sized luxury vehicle to a prospect who could only afford a sub compact model. By the same token, if your guest can afford the top of the line, go for it!

Most guests will have some areas of **concern.** It is the responsibility of the salesperson to make sure the concerns seem **insignificant** when compared to the long list of benefits.

People are most apt to become part of your program when they are assured other folks, **just like themselves,** had the same reservations, but decided to join and are now having the time of their lives.

When using **third party** stories, be sure the third party has **much in common** with your guests. Your third party might be the **same age,** live in the **same town,** or work at the **same** or similar **occupation.** It would be meaningless to tell a story about another owner with whom they could not relate.

The longer a salesperson practices his profession, the more third party stories he can recount to influence his guests. The rookie can garner his stories from the more experienced person, then simply preface his stories with "One of my associates had a couple just like you," or "My manager was telling me about some folks **just like yourselves,** who had the same problems as you do today. The way he helped those folks become part of the program was . . . "

Selling is a matter of **rearranging** your guests financial **priorities.** More often than not, they will be planning on making some major purchase in the near future, such as a home, a new car, or an addition to the old homestead.

The list of priorities your guests will have is endless. The guests will have their income committed for the kids college education, new furnishings, a new wardrobe, and on and on. The challenge to the salesperson is to create so much **need, want** and **desire** for his product that his guests will **rearrange** their priorities. They will put off buying the new car, hold off on the addition, or dip into the savings if they are convinced of the **value.**

Value can be built in several ways. In the case of deeded ownership of a week of interval ownership, the savings over a ten or twenty year period can be substantial, when compared to the cost of renting a hotel room for a like period. The cost of the deed is fixed, whereas hotel rates are subject to **inflation.**

Further savings can be realized by **free** or low cost use of recreation facilities in a resort. Compare to the annual cost of membership in a health spa or country club.

Building value can also involve **benefits** that will contribute to the general health of your guests. People who vacation regularly stay **healthier** and **live longer** than the workaholics. What value can be put on a longer, more rewarding life?

Value alone is not enough to prompt most to purchase, unless the value is reinforced by need, want, or desire for your product.

People **need** food, shelter and clothing for survival. These **basic physical requirements** are provided for all the inmates in our prison system. Obviously, satisfying basic physical needs does not necessarily contribute to happiness and does not do much to enhance the **quality** of our life.

A starving, homeless and poorly clothed vagrant might take exception to the previous statement, but the average American takes the basic **physical necessities** of life for **granted.**

Our psychological needs are quite a different story. For many, trying to satisfy psychological needs is a lifelong endeavor.

Many products are sold for ego satisfying reasons rather than their intrinsic value. Will your product give your guests more status, pride, security, love, friendship, money, companionship, fun, excitement, or recognition? Show them how it can satisfy any of these needs and you will move one step closer to the sale.

"**Variety** is the spice of life." This saying best illustrates the **difference** between **need** and **want.** What a dull life this would be if we had only those things that were absolutely necessary.

We don't **need** jewelry or luxury cars or spacious homes, or fun vacations to **exist.** We do, however, **want** and strive for the better life. In today's high pressure, fast moving, competitive society, fulfilling our **wants** can add to the quality of our lives by improving our overall sense of well being. Satisfied, happy people who take regular vacations live longer. For that reason alone, we **need** to have some of the **variety** we **want.**

Once you have created the **need** and **want** for our product, you must take the sale at least one step further and create **desire.** Desire is the strong emotion that creates a **sense of urgency to act now.** It will also **overwhelm the logic** that other priorities should come **first.**

Now that we have our guests' priorities rearranged, we are ready to close the sale.

CHAPTER FOUR

The Closing Process

Part I
The Mechanics Of The Closing Process

Reseat guests — **offer** refreshments.

Ask them if they have any questions about the program **up to this point.**

Answer questions — **highlight** high points of tour.

Summarize the total benefit package.

Show how inflation can work **for** them.

Overcome their fear and tension, if any.

Use agreements obtained as closing tools.

Show today prices and benefits. Disclose **all** costs.

Increase urgency.

Ask about the **order.** Upon affirmative response, **write** the **order.** If negative response, then

Smile and **harmonize** with objections.

Ignore minor objections, **isolate** and **overcome** major objections.

Appeal to higher authority.

Build credibility of, and **properly** introduce third party.

Have all paperwork clearly visible.

Save at least one major benefit for third party use.

Solidify sale.

Extract referral names from buyer.

Follow through with owner assurances and services.

Part II
The Methodology and Psychology
Of The Closing Process

Upon returning from your tour of the resort, seat your guests comfortably in the closing area. This is a good time to offer refreshments. It is preferable to have a **hostess** available to serve the refreshments. As a professional advisor, you should be **helpful** and **accommodating**, but **not subservient.**

Before offering any additional information (K.I.S.S.), ask your guests if they have any questions on the presentation **up to that point.**

Answer all the questions you can **completely** and **accurately** handle. Ask for **manager assistance** on any others. You will build credibility by impressing your guests with your **concern** that all answers be **correct.**

Summarize the total **benefit package.** Use graphics, color brochures and other sales aids to peak interest and desire.

Show how your guests will **save money** in the **long run.** Inflation is the **ally** of those who **own** something, and the **enemy** of those who **rent.**

Overcome any **fear** and **tension** by first listening **intently** to your guests' concerns, then offering calm, reassuring logic.

Recall all the **agreements** you obtained throughout the presentation and begin to close on **those** agreements. Guests are far more likely to buy based upon what **they said,** rather than what the **salesperson said.**

Now that you have built your guests to an emotional peak, **show prices,** prefacing the dollar amounts with **only** or **just.** Disclose **all** costs, including the **total** initial amount required **today.** Any **hidden** costs that turn up at a later date could well lead to **cancellation** of the contract. Review **again** all the benefits your guests will receive by joining **today.**

Increase the urgency of the offer with discounts, first day benefits, special inventory, supply and demand, and any other incentives that will give your guests the **excuse** or **reason** to **justify** taking action **now.**

Ask for the order. Don't sell **past the close.** Start writing the order in an **assumptive** manner. You **expect** them to take advantage, **today,** of this outstanding opportunity. **However,** should your guests respond negatively, or raise additional objections, simply **proceed** to the next step in the close.

How the guests are handled after the first **no** is what separates the professional **salesperson** from the **order taker.**

The first no is merely a signal to shift to second gear. **Never argue** with your guests. When you win the argument, you win the **battle,** but lose the **war. Always harmonize** with negative responses and objections. Never ridicule or embarrass your guests, regardless of how frivolous the objections may be. By letting your guests **save face,** you can **save the sale.**

> **EXAMPLES:**
> "I can see how you feel that way, John, however..."
> "What you say makes a lot of sense, Mary, but..."
>
> " Based upon the limited information you have at this point, I understand how you could come to that conclusion, however..."(add **new** information that will give your guests a **face saving** way to say **yes.**)

The professional salesperson will **anticipate** most common **objections** and be capable of **overcoming** the objections with logic or emotion, or a combination of both. Handling objections poorly is comparable to learning how to swim **half way** across a raging river. If you can't make it **all** the way across, with energy to spare, you are better off staying **on shore.** It is better to **realize your limitations** than to drown in a sea of confusion.

Minor objections may be ignored or simply acknowledged with body language. **If** they are **important** to your guests, they will raise the objection again. When the objection is raised the **second** time, it **must** be handled.

The salesperson who spends most of his time overcoming objections will be constantly on the **defensive.** He will also **lose control.** The time spent overcoming objections will detract from or eliminate a major portion of his presentation. How, then, do we decide which objections should be handled, and which should be ignored? The salesperson will have to use his own discretion. In each case he will have to determine which objections are petty excuses and can be ignored. Decide which are valid objections that must be handled in order to make the sale.

The real pro knows how to **separate excuses** from **reasons.** Most sales people, when given an objection, will go into a time consuming, lengthy oration in an attempt to overcome the objection. The pro will **first** find out whether it is a valid objection or just an excuse.

This can be accomplished with one word. **"Suppose?"** Let us assume the objection was distance. Our resort is one hundred miles from the closest major market area. So our prospect raises the objection, "It's too far". We could spend a half hour justifying the added driving time. Or, we could simply pose the hypothetical question, "Suppose our resort was thirty miles from your home, would you join?" If the answer was yes, we would try to overcome the distance objection. If the answer is, "No, I'd still have to check with my brother," you can see where the distance may **not** be the real reason. Possibly, checking with the brother is the real reason. We still would not try to overcome the second objection, **yet**. "Suppose our resort was thirty miles from your home, and your brother approved, would you join?" Now, the prospect bcomes a little uneasy and says, "I'd still have to go to my credit union for the down payment." Do we spend time on the credit union objection at this time? Of course not! How about, "Suppose our resort was thirty miles from your home, your brother approved, and the credit union had given you the money, would you join?" We could suppose forever until we finally extracted the **real reason.** This is seldom necessary as after the third or fourth excuse, it will be obvious to all the prospect is not being totally candid. He is grabbing at straws.

A tactful way to get to the real reason that your guest is reluctant to get involved would be a statement by the salesperson to this effect: "I have an obligation to give you a truthful and professional presentation of my product. You have no obligation whatsoever to purchase our product. However, I do believe you have an obligation to be totally honest with me. Now I ask, are the reasons you gave the **real reasons** you are hesitating to get involved in our community?" The response, after a short silence, will usually be the **real** reason.

Another commonly used term to determine if objections are valid is, "If I could, would you?" Let us suppose our guest complains about the financing terms. We could spend some time justifying our financing terms, only to have our guest raise another objection. A better way to handle this situation quickly would be for the salesperson to pose the question, "If I could get you better financing terms, would you join?" This would determine immediately if the financing terms were the major objection, or just another way to procrastinate.

In summary, **ignor petty excuses** and **concentrate** on the **major objections.** As a rule of thumb, no more than three or four of the objections raised should be addressed in detail. In the process of **narrowing** objections, **when narrowed** to one objection, the salesperson can confirm with the prospect, **"Is this the only thing** keeping you from getting involved today?" If the answer is yes, overcome that objection, and you will have a buying commitment in advance.

For **ways and means** to handle **specific** objections, refer to Chapter - **Overcoming Common Objections.**

There are times the best means to overcome an objection is to introduce a **third party** to the closing process. This third party could be anyone of **higher authority.**

Some sales people actually are **reluctant** to introduce a **third party** to assist in closing the sale. They mistakenly view a request for assistance as an admission they were incapable of closing the sale **by themselves.** The **experienced professional knows** there are times it is **wise** for the salesperson to request assistance. He laughs all the way to the bank at those who allow their **ego** to **reduce** their **paycheck.**

Exactly when we **appeal** to a **higher authority** depends upon the circumstances. Naturally, if the sale can be brought to a successful conclusion without assistance, by all means, write the order. You may still wish to have a higher authority **approve** the order.

Other reasons for introducing a third party include:
A. A personality conflict is often no fault of the salesperson. It may be the salesperson reminds his guests of **someone else,** in physical appearance or tone of voice, that the guests dislike or mistrust. The introduction of a "new face" may well be the answer.
B. The **aggressive salesperson** may have pressed a little too hard for the sale. The guests react to the **pressure** by becoming more closed and defensive. The third party, by assuming a more laid back and understanding posture, can lower defenses and depressurize the guests. Once this has been accomplished, the chances for a sale are greatly enhanced.

C. The most common reason for calling in a third party is to make a **credible change** from a previously **inflexible position.** The salesperson makes closing statements during the closing process from which he cannot retreat without losing credibility.

EXAMPLES:
A. "This is the lowest **price** at which we can sell this particular vacation package."
B. "This is the best **offer** we have available **today.**"
C. "We have only this **type** of inventory left."

The **third party** can give a **credible reason he** has a **lower price,** a **better offer** or **inventory** that was not available to his salesperson. The manager can also make some minor concessions that only a person of higher authority can make. The guests feel they received **special** consideration.

In resort sales, the higher authority, called in for assistance, is referred to as the **T.O.** The T.O. designation stands for **T**ake **O**ver. The name implies the salesperson should properly introduce the T.O., state under what **terms** and **conditions** his guests would join today, and then **remain quiet** while the T.O. assumes **control.**

Before calling in a T.O., the salesperson should build the qualifications and credibility of the T.O. Then the T.O. will receive the proper attention and respect from the guests.

By the time the T.O. is called upon for assistance, the salesperson should have been on a first name basis with his guests. The exception to the first name basis may be a professional or military title such as Doctor or Colonel.

Assuming the salesperson is on a first name basis with his guests, a proper introduction would be:
"John and Mary, I'd like you to meet Mr. Robert Smith, my manager. By using the surname of the T.O., you convey to your guests **your respect** for his position of **authority.** The T.O. can break the ice quickly by asking your guests to "call

be Bob." This is a quick method to show your manager is a warm, down to earth person.

Have the guests' completed vacation survey clearly visible to the T.O., as well as any financial figures you may have quoted. A fast glance at this information can provide the T.O. with some instant **insight** into your guests.

The salesperson who "gives away the farm" leaves little room for a T.O. to close the sale. At least one major benefit that can be offered to the guests should be reserved. Don't "shoot all the bullets" and hand the T.O. an empty gun. Some T.O.'s have learned to walk on water, but only in the Winter when the lake is *frozen!* From the time of signing of the agreements to the departure of the new buyers, the salesperson should:

    A. Be **calm** and **reassuring**

    B. **Explain** all paperwork thoroughly in simple **layman's** terms.

    C. Be sure all documents are properly executed and all figures contained therein are correct.

Extract names of the new buyers' friends, relatives, coworkers, whom they feel would quality for, and benefit from, the program. Also:

    A. Offer **congratulations** and a promise to be in touch **shortly** to answer any additional questions they may have or perform some service on their behalf.

    B. Give a temporary member card or auto window sticker to new owners as a **symbol** to reinforce their commitment.

Follow up with a phone call to new owners. Flowers or some token gift to welcome them aboard will go a long way towards **raising** your new buyers' **confidence level** and reducing their **buyers' remorse.**

Buy understanding the **questions** your new buyers are likely to **ask themselves after the sale,** you can make sure your sales presentation provides a **yes** answer to all the most common concerns:

    A. "Do I trust the company and person from whom I purchased?"

    B. "Do I really **need** this product?"

    C. "Does my purchase fit my **budget** and **lifestyle**?"

    D. "Will my purchase help **solve** any of my present or future vacation problems?"

    E. "Were the first day benefits **worth** moving so quickly?"

    F. "Do the **benefits** far outweigh the **risk?**"

    G. "Are we convinced we could not have better by **shopping** further?"

The **satisfied, properly serviced** buyer is the **best** source of referrals. Referral sales are the easiest sale for the resort salesperson. Word of mouth has already built **credibility** and **trust** in you and your product. Salespersons who follow up and properly service their buyers are the perfect example of **people who work smart — not hard.**

Overcoming Objections

The salesperson should perceive objections as **excellent closing tools.** Only those with a conscious, or possible subconscious, **interest** in your offer have reason to raise objections.

The major **problem** with **objections** lies between the ears of some sales people. Most objections are **stated negatively.** However, by **hearing** them in a **positive** manner, they can be converted into **trial closes.**

Examples:

Objection: "The unit is too small."

Hear as: "I would buy if units were larger."

Two opportunities to close:

A.   Switch to a larger unit, or

B.   Justify why this size unit would probably be adequate.

Objection: "This unit is too expensive."

Hear as: "I would buy if this unit were less expensive."

Two opportunities to close:

A.   Switch to a less expensive unit, or

B.   Justify price (value) of the unit.

*Objection: "Your resort is **too far**."*

Hear as: "I would buy if the resort were closer."

While we cannot move the resort to accommodate our guests, we can **isolate** this objection with — "Is the driving distance the **only thing** keeping you from joining today?" If the answer is **yes,** every salesperson should have a **list** of reasons **their** resort is **worth** the added travel time.

Now, on to some suggested **guidelines** for overcoming the most **common** objections. Your common sense and creativity will tell you when you should **deviate** from these **proven techniques.**

Objection: "I want to think about it."

When guests have not been allowed **mental pauses** during the presentation, they cannot absorb all the information. It is then natural for them to "want to think about it." **Simplifying and slowing down** your presentation will help. So will summarizing the important points as often as necessary.

Another common reason for "I have to think about it" is doubt in the mind of the buyer about the product or the salesperson. They are not convinced it is the "fantastic opportunity" it is purported to be. Use more written documentation to increase your believability. Also, review your total presentation, looking for areas where you could strengthen your credibility.

Method # 1 — To overcome this objection, it is pointless to say, "What is it you wish to think about?" More than likely the answer will be "Everything." You have accomplished nothing. A better approach would be to say, "Is it the unit you have to think about?" "No." "Is it the beach you have to think about?" "No." "Is it the financing terms?" "No." Each succeeding "no" only **proves** they have already considered most of the important points. When finally a "yes" is received, you have narrowed it to an objection that can be handled.

Method # 2 — "Doesn't it make sense to think about and discuss it **here?** At home you will not have an expert to field your questions. Any questions that arise **here** can be answered immediately. Those answers could assist you in arriving at an intelligent decision. More important, this unit could be sold by the time you do make a **"choice."**

Method # 3 — Intellectuals will usually want to think it over first. Excerpts from studies show most very successful people reach decisions promptly, and seldom change their decisions.

Procrastination is the source of much personal and business failure. Ironically, those who take the longest to reach a decision are the quickest to change it. Give one of these excerpts to the intellectual to read. It could motivate him to act now.

Method # 4 — "I knew you would want to think about it. Most intelligent people **do** want to carefully weigh important matters. **However,** today is your **sale day.** That means our offer is more **attractive today** than any time in the **future.** To get the most **value** for our dollars, the best time to buy things we want is when they are on sale. That makes a lot of sense, doesn't it?"

Objection: "I never make a decision the same day."

"I can understand that. Possibly, you have not come across an opportunity as outstanding as the one I'm offering today. However, if you think long enough, possibly you will recall some other tremendous opportunity you decided upon the same day. **Couldn't you?"**

Your guests will either admit they did make some other purchase on the first day, or, they could recall how they got burned by rushing into some other situation. "The real problem was not making a prompt decision, but rather the product was misrepresented to you. Isn't that so?" A yes and you are half way home. A disagreement opens new dialogue and other opportunities to close.

The salesperson must be persistent in the pursuit of a sale. Many give up too quickly. Be like the fireman who was giving mouth-to-mouth resuscitation to a victim of smoke inhalation. Another fireman leaned over and said, "You **can't help** that man, he's dead." The fireman attempting to revive the apparently dead victim replied, "If you are right, I sure **can't hurt** him." He continued with his efforts. The victim slowly and miraculously came to life. So can your guests!

Objection: "I can't afford it."

"You can't afford to **wait.** Prices have been increasing at a faster rate than you could **save.** I realize it may stretch your budget today, but can you afford to run the risk of the unit being priced totally out of your range in the future?"

Method # 2 — "This could be your way to added financial security by building equity in your deed. Somehow, you must find the means to take advantage of this opportunity. It may not be easy, but do you know of anything worthwhile in life that is easy to come by?"

Method # 3 — "I can't afford it" could also mean the salesperson did not properly qualify his guests for affordability. He has shown inventory beyond their means.

When this situation occurs, the salesperson is forced to drop from the "top of the line" to something more affordable. He **must** tactfully **justify** how the lower priced inventory will **still** serve their needs. He can show it has some exceptional features of its own.

Example:

A. "This luxury, full size car affords more room and a softer ride, **but** the sub-compact gets far better mileage and has **lower upkeep.**"

B. "The luxury two-bedroom unit accommodates more people, but the initial cost and annual maintenance of an efficiency unit is far less."

Objection: "We are considering a resort closer to home."

Know your competition well. What resorts are any closer to your guests home? What are their prices? Are they overcrowded, or still within the air pollution zone of a major city? A quality vacation in a private, clean, uncrowded environment is well worth the extra driving time.

If your prices are **lower** than your competitors, you could use the price difference to **offset transportation costs.**

To **dramatize** the importance of **prime** location, you could pose this **choice:**

"Assuming you had a choice between a week's vacation in a crowded slum area that was just **one half hour** from your home, or a lovely country setting that looked like the "Garden of Eden," **two hours** from your home, where would you rather go?"

When your guests choose the obvious "Garden of Eden" vacation, you can **then** respond — "Obviously, the **quality** of a vacation, **after** you arrive, is far more significant than the driving distance, don't you agree?"

Objection: "I'll buy when I get caught up on my bills."

"I realize you would have to make some sacrifices to purchase at this time. However, there **never** is a convenient time to buy. Prime real estate usually appreciates faster than you could save. The best time to buy is now, before it is priced out of your reach."

Method # 2 — "Have you ever walked through a cemetery and read the inscriptions on the tombstones? You will never see an inscription that reads, "He was never late paying his bills." You will, however, see many inscriptions that read "He was a good father" or "She was a loving mother." It's a matter of rearranging your priorities."

Method # 3 — "Pretend you took your family to the movies. You sat next to your banker, your insurance broker, and your car dealer. If a fire broke out, would you save the banker, the insurance broker and car dealer **first,** then, if time permitted, come back to rescue your **family?"**

"Of course not! You would put your family ahead of everyone else. That's what we are talking about today."

"This program is not just another bill. It's a commitment to **pay yourself first.** Don't you think that ten (10) percent of your gross earnings is a small amount to set aside to assure a lifetime of quality vacations for you and your family?"

> *Objection: "We are too old."*

"A recent study stated persons who remain active and live in pleasant, clean surroundings live as much as seven years longer. What is a year of your life worth?"

Method # 2 — "This is an excellent legacy for your children and grandchildren. Unlike cash, it cannot be easily squandered."

> *Objection: "We have to check with the children."*

Find out **up front** if there is anyone your guests would have to check with in order to make a **choice today.** This allows **more time** to overcome the objection.

Method # 2 — "Who knows the likes and dislikes of your children better than you? Is there **anything** about our resort you feel they may **not** enjoy? For a substantial portion of your childrens' lives, **you** made all the decisions for them. I'm sure there is nobody's judgment in this world your children trust more than yours. So why not go ahead with this program **today.** Your children will love you for it."

Objection: "I have to check with my parents."

Appeal to the self respect and sense of independence of younger couples. Comments like, "It is a pleasure to deal with young people who know their **own** mind."

Method # 2 — "Learning to make decisions early in life will help you in succeeding in the business world. A study of the most successful executives in this country revealed they had one characteristic in common. They all had the ability to make a prompt decision. Not only do they make prompt decisions, but they have the self confidence to stick with their decision. This is why I know you are going to be very successful."

Objection: "I want to check with my attorney or accountant first."

"Every purchaser has a period in which to cancel the contract. This time is provided for you and your attorney or accountant to review the condominium documents and all the contracts. If **you** are making the decision to purchase, and your lawyer or accountant is just **checking** the paperwork for **legality** and **accuracy,** we should be able to do business today."

This method is called **reverse** selling or **doing a take-away.**

The salesperson who uses the rescission period as a sales tool, without extracting a **moral commitment** from the buyer, is selling weak and will suffer a high cancellation rate.

Method # 2 — "May I ask you a question? **Without** the information received over the past two hours, and the tour through our resort, could **you** have made an informed recommendation to **anyone** as to the merits of our program?" Upon receiving an honest **no,** you pose the key question: "Does it make sense to trust your **future** to anyone who knows **less** about the program than **you** do?"

Objection: "We don't need it."

"Wouldn't it be a dull world if we only had the things we absolutely need? Did you ever hear the story of the man stranded on the hot burning desert? After miles of crawling over sand dunes, he spotted a little booth that looked like a refreshment stand. "Water, water," he cried, as he rushed toward the booth. Much to his surprise and dismay, it was not a refreshment stand. The man in the booth was selling ties. "We have an excellent assortment of ties for five dollars," the man in the booth said. "Are you crazy?" shouted the stranded man. "I want water, I don't need a tie."

"Many miles further across the burning sand, he sees in the distance an unbelievable sight. A tropical, posh oasis with an elaborate building surrounded by a high iron fence. A flashing neon sign reads, "Pierre's Restaurant." "Thank God, I'm saved," thought the dying man. Almost too weak to crawl, too parched to talk, he uses his last ounce of strength to reach the high iron gate. A sign reads, "Push bell for service." He anxiously pushes the bell and a waiter, dressed in a tuxedo, appears. "Let me in," gasps the dying man, "I want water." To which the waiter replies, "I'm sorry sir, we can't let you in without a tie!"

"You never know when you will need something!"

Method # 2 — Prisoners have everything they need. Their major punishment is that they cannot **travel.** This is luxury you both **deserve,** and **need** as well, if you consider **health** and **happiness** as part of our basic needs.

> *Objection: "I want a large penthouse suite. We can't afford it at this time, but we will settle for nothing less."*

"There is absolutely nothing wrong with **wanting** the best. However, you must be realistic. "Do you live in a mansion, drive a Rolls Royce, wear **all** the latest designer fashions?" "No?" These are all things people want, but have learned to live within their means. Why should your vacation be any different? Take advantage of all the first day benefits by purchasing the studio unit **today.** Enjoy it until the penthouse is affordable. That makes sense, doesn't it?"

> *Objection: "I didn't come prepared to buy. I left my cash, checkbook, and credit cards at home."*

"If you had the means with you today, would you get involved?" If the answer is yes, we respond, "Fine, we can do the paperwork now; I'll follow you home to pick up the check." If the objection was genuine, we have a sale. If not, it was just another excuse. Continue probing for the **real reason.**

> *Objection: "The interest rate is too high."*

"I can see why you might think the interest rate is too high. Our company had two options. The first choice was to set a higher base price and lower the interest rate. The second choice was to lower the base price and raise the interest rate. In both cases, your cost would be identical. Our firm chose the second option, because **only** the interest portion of your loan is tax deductible. This way, our owners have a bigger tax benefit. This gives our company the same revenue, but lowers the **net** to you. That makes sense, doesn't it?"

> *Objection: "Your prices are too high."*

Justify prices and compare to higher priced, less desirable competition.

Method # 2 — Explain the difference between **price** and **cost.** Show your product actually **costs less** because of equity savings in the deed.

Method # 3 — "Suppose our prices were lower, would you join today?" If answered affirmatively, seek lower priced inventory. If necessary, use a T.O. to maintain **credibility.**

Objection: "I don't want to cash my Certificates of Deposit (C.D.'s)."

"Have you ever heard of one millionaire who said, 'I made all my money in bank interest'? Probably not. Know why? Most bank interest is fully taxable. After reducing bank interest by taxes, next we must adjust the net return for inflation. This could leave you with a **paper profit,** but a **net loss** in real **purchasing power.**"

"With timeshare, a ten percent down payment will buy a unit valued at ten times your initial cash investment. This is the principle of leverage. You earn a return on ten dollars for every one dollar you invest. Also, interest on loans, for those who itemize, may be deductible."

"You can't **spend** money here. You can transfer funds from the savings bank to the real estate bank. No **guaranteed** low interest return, but the probability of an **excellent** return, plus **use** and **enjoyment** of the unit."

Method # 2 — "Leave your Certificates of Deposit in the bank, but borrow against them. Borrow enough to cover the initial down payment and closing costs. If your budget is tight, also borrow enough to cover the monthly installments due until the Certificate matures. Secured loans of this nature are usually made at just a few percent more than you are receiving on the Certificate of Deposit. The loan cost would be far **less than** the **savings** you will realize today.

*Objection: "I would join **today**, but my wife does not want to get involved at this time."*

Ask the wife what **she** would buy if given the same amount of money as the down payment. If she responds her first priority is a new freezer, carpeting, a fur coat, or any other item, turn to the husband and say, "If your wife goes along with you today, will you buy her the freezer, the carpeting, the fur coat, (etc.) that she has been wanting?" In many cases, the husband will say yes. Now both parties are happy. This is known as the trade-off close. Naturally, this close can be used if their positions were reversed.

Method # 2 — Try a "divide-and-conquer" close. Reason with the **positive** partner that they work hard and deserve to have what they want. This type of close should be used only as a last resort, and only with a high degree of finesse. The primary goal is to get the sale. It would be a stronger sale if both were in complete harmony and accord. However, when you **can't sell both, sell one.**

Objection: "I'm too busy to take a vacation."

"Even the Lord stopped and rested on the seventh day. Life is not a dress rehearsal. Stop and smell the roses. No one knows just how long we will be on earth. We owe it to ourselves and our family to enjoy life now."

Method # 2 — When the husband is a workaholic, you could say to the wife, "I'm sure you would rather be a happy wife than a rich widow. Get your hubby away from the rat race. You need a retreat to spend some time **together.**"

Ask your guests when they last had the oil changed in their car, or made repairs to their home. "Should you take better care of your house and car than you do of yourselves? Without each other, how important are the home and car? Put yourselves first!"

Objection: "What if — I lose my job?" — "What

*if — I get transferred?" — "What if — I incur
unexpected medical expenses?" — "What if —
(all others)."*

"What if you are hit by **lightning** on the way home, or your
car is hit by a train? You won't need the unit then either,
would you? To purchase today, you need to have a relatively
positive attitude about the **future.**"

"When you purchased your home, you had no guarantee
against job loss, becoming ill, nor any other concerns. What
then, prompted you to risk purchasing a home? I'm sure you
realized you were really risking **nothing.** If you did not own,
your alternative was to pay an ever increasing amount of **rent.**
The only thing you would do is accumulate a drawer full of
useless rent receipts."

"If it makes sense to **own** your own **home,** doesn't it make
just as much sense to **own** your own **vacation.?**"

Objection: "We want to shop first."

"If it was a car or appliance being considered, shopping
would make sense. In a number of different locations the
identical products are sold. The dealer with the best price
and service would probably be the best place to buy.
Resorts, on the other hand, are **unique.** Each resort has its
own **character** and **location.** The unit you inspected cannot
be purchased anywhere else. While shopping, it could be
sold. The best buys go to those who **take action.** The
average buy goes to the shoppers. You know this unit is an
excellent value. Are you willing to risk losing it, on the **slim
possibility** that something comparable might be over the
horizon?"

Objection: "I have to pray on it."

The wishes of preachers, ministers and other deeply religious
persons who genuinely wish to pray for divine guidance in
reaching a decision should be respected and their religious
beliefs honored.

However, logic may assist them in taking a more realistic and humble approach to reaching a decision.

Without being sacrilegious, point out to the preacher or minister this logic: "There are wars, famine, pestilence and other worldwide problems. Do you honestly feel **God** should decide whether you should purchase a unit? **God** gave you a **free will,** to make decisions that, while important, to **you,** are **not** of **universal** concern."

"Before we appeal to the Lord for assistance on everyday decisions, don't you think we should **first try** our **free will,** the gift the Lord has given us for that purpose?"

Preachers are used to **giving,** not **accepting,** good advice. A high degree of tact, diplomacy, and finesse is required when we discuss matters of religious convictions.

Objection: "We may not be able to sell our unit."

While this statement could prove to be true in times of poor economic conditions, the number of units in the development should be compared to the total number of **potential** prospects in the market area. Know the demographics of the market area. On a map, draw a line between the three closest major population areas. This can be referred to as the **Golden Triangle.** "Within this area there are millions of families that could use a vacation hideaway. Our resort has only a fixed number of units. While demand may rise and fall, the trend for decades has been generally **upward.** The greater the demand, the easier to sell. You do see that, don't you?"

Objection: "We don't make snap decisions."

Print the word **SNAP** in large, bold letters on a blank sheet of paper. Show it to your guests. "Do you know what **that word means to me?"** Draw two lines through the letter S to form a dollar sign. "What it says now, is that while some people nap, others make dollars."

Method # 2 — Show preprinted materials from studies that document **indecision** is a far greater cause of **failure** than wrong decisions. **Successful** people move quickly when an exceptional offer is presented.

> *Objection: "I'm just not interested."*

Rekindle interest by **reselling** features, benefits, and value of the program.

Try **lower priced** inventory. Sometimes "not interested" is a **face saving** way to say **"can't afford."**

There may be built up **pressure** or a **personality conflict.** Try introducing a third party.

> *Objection: "We would not use it."*

"Several months ago I met a couple, **just like yourselves,** whose major concern was that they **wouldn't use it.** When they finally realized owning a vacation unit would **force** them to **save money** and **take** much needed **vacations,** they decided to join.

"The very next week, I came across that couple at our poolside **restaurant** having a relaxing lunch. The week after, I saw them at the swimming pool. The third week I ran into them again at the **health club,** I couldn't resist saying, **"I see you're not using it again."** They laughed and thanked me for my help.

"There is little doubt in my mind, that you **could** and **would** get just as much **use** and **enjoyment** from our program as that couple. Don't you agree?"

> *Objection: "It's more than we care to invest."*

Step # 1 — Write down the sale price of your product.

Step # 2 — Determine **how much** your guest **is** willing to invest; deduct that amount from sale price.

Step # 3 — Determine the **monthly** installment required to finance the **difference** (result of Step # 2).

Step # 4 — Divide **monthly** installment amount in Step # 3 by 30 (days). The result = cost **per day.**

> **Example:**
>
> | | |
> |---|---|
> | Step # 1 — Price of unit week | $10,000 |
> | Step # 2 — (Less) amount Guests willing to invest | $ 8,000 |
> | Step # 3 — Difference | $ 2,000 |
> | Step # 4 — Monthly installment on $2,000 financed for 10 years @ 15% APR | $32.26 Mo. |
> | $32.26/month divided by 30 = | $ 1.08 Day |

Less than the price of a pack of **cigarettes!** — For a lifetime of luxury vacations.

> *Objection: "I never vacation in one place for a full week at a time."*

"People who own a vacation home, on the average, seldom use it more than 10 to 20 weeks per year. The balance of the year, they either leave it unoccupied or offer it for rent.

"The heavy cash flow to maintain a second home 52 weeks each year could **exceed** the cost of a **rented** vacation. However, this is offset by the buildup in **equity** and **inflationary increases** in the resale value of the home. In some very popular areas with a healthy economy, the owner could receive a **total return** of his investment, plus a **profit** also.

So it is with a week of deeded vacation ownership. You are free to use your week in **whole** or **part.** Those families who use only the weekends have the same type options available as the second home owner. Once the unit has been paid in full, the **cash flow** requirements drop sharply. At a time hotel and motel rates are constantly rising, the owner of a paid-in-full deeded vacation week is **then** only obligated to pay a **nominal** maintenance fee.

In future years, the deed may well have a resale value equal to, or exceeding, the total of all dollars invested. The owner may elect to keep his unit, pass it on to future generations, or resell it to recover his equity.

In summation, it makes as much sense for the interval owner to use 2 or 3 days each year of the week he owns, as it does for the vacation home owner to use 10 to 20 weeks of the 52 weeks he owns. "Don't you agree?"

Method # 2 — "You may be like other families who do not feel comfortable spending a week in a small hotel room. With your vacation unit, you have kitchen facilities and more of the comforts of home. You may now **enjoy** a week's stay in one location."

Method # 3 — "As a member of the exchange service, many of the resorts listed offer daily and weekend rentals at very competitive rates."

> *Objection: "We have a motor home and enjoy traveling."*

"Many of our owners have motor homes. A wonderful way to see our beautiful country is to select a vacation resort **in the center** of the general area you would like to visit. Then, every morning, start out on a new adventure, visiting areas within a few hours' ride of the resort. Every evening, return to relax in the **luxury** of your home resort. Each year you can select another exciting vacation location."

Objection: "We enjoy camping."

"That's understandable. Roughing it in the great outdoors can be lots of fun. But don't you think you deserve at least **one week** of **luxury** vacations each year? Convert some of the money you are **spending** on camping to **equity** in a deeded week of vacation ownership."

Stress those timeshare unit benefits **least likely** to be found on a camping vacation. Items such as **spacious** accommodations, color **cable** T.V., jacuzzis, and **fully** equipped kitchens can be a refreshing **change** from campfires and biting insects.

Another method of handling an objection is to **repeat the objection** back to your guests, but in the form of a **question.**

Example:

Guests — "We are not convinced of the value."

Salesperson's response — "You are not convinced of the value?" — followed by silence.

This approach forces the guests to **justify why** they feel the way they do. The added information will provide more guidance as to **how** to convince your guests of the **value.**

Additional Closes

ALTERNATE CHOICE CLOSE

Instead of asking a question that requires a yes or no answer, give your guests a **choice** of two positive alternatives. Either answer is a commitment to purchase.

Example:
A. "Would you prefer the one bedroom **or** two bedroom unit?"
B. "Do you prefer to pay cash **or** take advantage of our liberal financing plan?"
C. "Will you be using a personal check **or** your credit card?"

BEN FRANKLIN CLOSE

When Ben wanted to make a decision about any important matter, he listed all the pros and cons on a sheet of paper. Based upon whichever list was longer, pro or con, he would decide for or against. Suggest your guests use the same method today. With your **help**, the list of buying reasons will be substantially **longer.**

ASSUMPTIVE CLOSE

Assume the sale by proceding to fill out the purchase order in a **matter of fact** manner.

Appropriate questions for an assumptive close are:

A. "Will you be vacationing **here** this year, or **elsewhere** through the exchange service?"
B. "Would you prefer to have **both** names on the deed?"

APOLOGY CLOSE

When all **dialogue** has been **exhausted,** a last resort is the apology close. "Mary and John, I owe you an **apology.** Somewhere along the line, I must have omitted some important information, or left room for doubt. We both know our resort suits your needs perfectly. **What else could it be?**" They will offer assurance that you **did** indeed cover all the points thoroughly. **"It's just that we,"** — and here you have the **real objection.** Overcome **that** objection, and you're **back in the ball game!**

SALE CONTEST CLOSE

Whenever your guests are offered very special terms or a sharply discounted price, it is vital a **credible** reason is given for any concession made.

People will accept and believe your actions quicker if told you have a **selfish** motive. "With just **one** more sale, I win a trip to Hawaii," — will **justify why** you were willing to make such an exceptional offer.

AGREEMENT CLOSE

Make a positive statement about an **area** of general agreement with your guests. Ask your guests **why** they agree on that particular point. When they have responded, assume the sale based upon **that** agreement.

INDIRECT CLOSE

When showing the **final** sales price and terms, the pressure on the guests can be lowered by asking:

"How do you **feel** about this?"

or

"How does this **look** to you?"

This softer, more **subtle** approach gives your guests the opportunity to say **yes** to the offer, **or** discuss any reservations they may still have. "Do you want to buy this?" tends to **force** a straight yes or no answer. This leaves little room for dialogue if your guests are not ready **yet** to commit.

THE REFERRAL CLOSE

People understand the philosophy behind the saying, "One hand washes the other," or "You do something for me, and I'll do something for you."

The best **way to justify** special concessions made to new buyers is by asking them for a list of **referrals at time of close.**

"By giving us the names of five (5) nice families, as qualified as yourselves, you save our company marketing costs. In turn, **what I'll do for you is . . ."** (special price, terms, etc.)

REPORT CARD CLOSE

When the sale appears lost, and your guests are **resistant** to the introduction of a third party, the report card close can be effective.

The salesperson appears **resigned** to the fact his guests are not buying today. He informs them, "The presentation is **over,** but there is **one** more step that must be taken before you can be on your way. A manager must confirm with you that I have done a credible and professional job."

In the minds of the guests, the manager is coming to the table **only** to do a "report card" on the **salesperson.** Therefore, they lower their resistance level.

After the introduction, the (T.O.) manager would ask questions such as:

A. "Did your salesperson explain everything to your satisfaction?"

B. "Did he show you the . . ." (list key amenities such as, pool, tennis courts, etc.)

C. "Did he show you the model units?"

D.   "Did he explain the exchange program properly?"
When the guests respond positively, the T.O. has subtly
completed a **summary close.** He would then ask, — "If your
salesperson **has** done such a commendable job, would you
mind sharing with me **exactly** why you are not joining us
today?" Whatever the response, the **possibility** of a sale is
kept alive. The answer affords the **manager** an opportunity
to employ **different** techniques to close the sale.

TRY IT CLOSE

When the potential buyer is **reluctant** to enter into any **long
term** financial obligation, the salesperson **can** suggest a
lesser commitment to the program by injecting the words
try it.

"Try it" implies something less than a **permanent** obligation
to own the product. **If** the buyer decides the vacation is not
suited to his lifestyle, or experiences any financial problems,
the **deed** can be **sold** or **transferred.**

The **liquidity** of the deed is often dictated by national
economic conditions and **local demand.** Therefore, the
salesperson should exercise **care** in providing the buyer with
a **realistic** assessment of the **resale potential** of the product.

PERSONAL CHOICE CLOSE

"Mary and John, when you are on vacation, driving down
the highway, do you call your accountant or attorney to ask
where you should stop for the night? Your vacations are a
matter of **personal preference,** not an accounting or legal
problem. Your choice today is no different, **wouldn't you
agree?"**

SAFE DEPOSIT CLOSE

"Mary and John, put the figures you were quoted today in a
safe deposit box. Ten years from today, have your children
look at the offer to see what you **could have** provided for
them at today's prices. Do you **really** think they will agree
with your decision to pass up **this** offer today?"

CRADLE TO THE GRAVE CLOSE
"Mary and John, there is never a **convenient** time to buy.

Young couples tell they can't buy **now,** because they are **getting married.**

The same couple can't buy **later** because they are **having children.**

Next they can't buy because they are saving for the kids' **college education.**

Finally, they can't buy because they are **too old.**

Life is not a dress rehearsal. We only go around once. Stop and smell the roses. Do it **now?**"

SAVE MONEY CLOSE
"Do you see where this program would **save** you **money?**"

"Are you interested in **saving money?**"

"When would be the best time to **start saving money?**"

CHAPTER SEVEN

The Sales Smorgasbord*

* Smorgasbord — *"A wide variety of appetizers
and tasty food served buffet style."*

Just as a food **buffet** allows each individual to select the
food that **he** prefers, so does this sales smorgasbord allow
each salesperson to select the information and sales techniques
that best suit **his** style and personality.

This **"food for the mind"** was **not** included in the basic sales
presentation in keeping with the K.I.S.S. philosophy. The
number of sales methods that **could be** applied is virtually
limitless. Each new sales situation poses a new opportunity
for **creativity.**

Inserted in the proper place, at the proper time, the
following material will enhance your ability to **close** more
sales.

For reference, each item on the sales menu is listed under the
general sales topic to which it can be most effectively
applied.

INVESTMENT

Most forms of **prime** real estate have proven to be a good
long term investment. However, the only **guarantees** in life
are **death** and **taxes.** Therefore, the ethical salesperson
restricts his presentation to the most important investment
his guests can make, an investment in their **own health** and
happiness.

While you cannot solve the problems of death and **taxes,**
you certainly can improve the situation. Financing **interest**
may be **tax deductible,** and persons who "stop to smell the
roses," **live longer.**

For those who constantly worry about the **future,** and in the process let life slip through their fingers, remind them, "You never see an armored car following a funeral procession." "You only go around once," is the old saying. For those who do it right the first time, once may be enough.

PREJUDGING

Shabby clothes still have **pockets.** Don't judge a book by its cover. Thousands of stories are related throughout the sales profession about the shabbily dressed customer who, after being spurned and ignored by the **amateur, "bought out the store"** from the **professional.**

SELLING PAST THE CLOSE

Continuing to sell **after** you have purchase commitment creates **doubt** in the mind of the potential buyer. **Why,** if your product is so outstanding, would you feel the **need** to **continue** extolling the benefits of your product after they have said yes. The **seed of doubt** grows into the **tree** of **apprehension** and **fear.** The only **fruit** that tree bears is **cancellation.**

Calm reassurance, congratulations, and a commitment of follow up service to assure buyer satisfaction, are the **only** requirements to **"button up"** the sale after the buying commitment.

SELLING WITH LOGIC

While **every** sale must contain **sufficient** logic to justify the selling price and give the buyer bona fide reasons to become part of the program, a presentation must **stir the emotions** of the guests in order to move them to action.

Fun filled days, basking in the warm sun, romantic nights dancing under the stars, dining overlooking the pounding surf, or a moonlit walk along a secluded beach paint colorful mental pictures that will help them visualize the years of enjoyment they will have by becoming part of the program.

Remember this simple formula:

Logic = Think   Emotion = Action

THE RIGHT ATTITUDE

Sales people who do not **believe** in their product generally feel they are doing something **to** the buyer, rather than **for** the buyer.

The career professional **knows** if he **helps** fill the **real** needs of his guests, he performs a valuable **service,** and at the same time assures his **own** success. Survey most top sales professionals and you will find sales to referrals from satisfied owners generate a large portion of their income. **Helping** others get what they need is the surest way of getting what **you need!**

TELL IT ALL

One of the quickest ways to lose a sale is for the buyer to become aware of hidden or undisclosed charges and expenses **after** the sale has been closed.

The dollar amount of the undisclosed amount is not the relevant issue. The buyer who finds out, after agreement, that there will be **any** added expense, inevitably asks himself, "What **other** charges are there which have not been disclosed?"

When listing all charges, it is better to state the **total** amount **first,** followed quickly by a **list** of all the charges **included** in the total.

While the dollar amount is the same, it is psychologically better to **justify** the **largest** amount by **reducing** it by all the items it includes, than to start with a small single item amount, and **increase** that amount, item by item.

SELL THE RIGHT ONE AND HUNDREDS WILL BUY

Many sales people are so busy trying to sell their guests that

they forget to sell the most important person of all
—**themselves.**

When a salesperson sells himself **totally** on his product,
genuine enthusiasm and **conviction** become a **natural** part
of his presentation. He then possesses the "exalted look of
the believer." Conviction breeds **trust,** and **trust** is the
cornerstone of all sales.

THE FEEL, FELT, FOUND METHOD
Another way to **harmonize** with the objections of your
guests is to respond that:

    A. "I know how you **feel.**"
    B. "I've **felt** that way myself."
    C. "But once I had **all** the information, I
    found—"(Add your reasoning why their objection
    is either not valid or insignificant.)

PRICE VS COST
Who among us has not succumbed to the temptation to
purchase something **just because** it was "on sale" at an
irresistibly low price?

The drawer full of cosmetics, the ill fitting shoes, the cheap
looking suit or pants, and the faulty kitchen appliance are
all physical evidence of our weakness to put **price** before **real
cost** or **value.**

**The lesson to be learned is that we can pay too little for some
things. Quality** items that stand the test of time are almost
always priced higher, but **cost** far less in the long run.

Example:

	Compact Car #1	Luxury Car #2
Purchase **price**	$10,000	$20,000
Average useful life	4 yrs.	10 yrs.
Cost per year	$ 2,500	$ 2,500

Quality *saves* money — live better at lower **cost.**

BREAKING THE SALES SLUMP

To the professional salesperson, a prolonged **sales slump** can be discouraging and depressing. Unfortunately, it is an experience almost all sales people have to weather periodically during their career. The **causes** of sales slumps are varied. However, there are **certain common denominators** that **trigger** most sales slumps. Once the sales slump exceeds a few days, a **negative** change in the **attitude** and **delivery** of the salesperson can **sustain** and **compound** the problem.

By **recognizing** the causes, the career professional can **minimize** the **frequency** and **severity** of sales slumps.

COMMON CAUSES OF THE SALES SLUMP

A. Preoccupation with **outside** interests and/or **personal** or **financial problems.**

B. Adding too much information to presentation.

C. Failure to **allow** guests sufficient **time** to **absorb presentation.**

D. **Prejudging,** rather than qualifying, guests.

E. **Constantly changing** your presentation to that of whichever of your peers is selling successfully **at the moment.**

F. **Complacency** - "resting on your past laurels."

G. Failure to be **objective** about your lack of sales.

H. Loss of self confidence - over analysis.

COMMON CURES FOR THE SALES SLUMP

A. **Check your problems** at the front desk at the start of every business day. **Convince yourself** that worrying about your problems, during working hours can only compound your problems, and in extreme cases, threaten your job security.

Motivational music and tapes enroute to work, followed by association with positive thinking people, can help you separate your personal and business life.

B. Tape your presentation periodically. Compare your **current** presentation to the presentation you **were** giving when you were most successful. Have you added "the staw that broke the camel's back to presentation? Remember K.I.S.S.

C. Allow "mental pauses" for your guests to absorb your presentation.

D. Don't **prejudge** any guests. Look for the means to **qualify** your guests to **become** your newest owners, rather than looking for ways to **justify** why you did not make the sale.

E. While it is wise to **observe** and **learn** from those who are successful, the **goal** of every sales professional should be to develop a strong, consistent sales presentation in which they have confidence. Changes should be made slowly and with much caution. In this manner, you can perfect a presentation that is effective and best suited to **your** personality.

By "grabbing at straws", and changing your total presentation frequently, your chances of perfecting **any** presentation are slim.

F. **Complacency** can lead to a boring monotone and "canned" presentation. The pro realizes he must **make** things happen, rather than coast along, **waiting** for things to happen.

G. **Objectively** analyze your **recent** performance. Some sales people perpetuate a slump by **blaming everyone** and **everything else** for their lack of production. Lack of **any self analysis** greatly reduces the chances of getting to the root of the sales problem.

H.Over analysis, known as **"paralysis of analysis,"** can be more destructive than too little self analysis. Make a **reasonable** review of your past presentations, mentally correcting any mistakes you feel you made. Then put the errors out of your mind and assume you will not make the same mistakes again. **Dwelling** on **lost** sales can only detract from your performance.

Possibly there were no buyers among your last string of guests. The salesperson who delivers a consistent, well planned and properly delivered presentation is seldom plagued with **doubt** and loss of **self confidence.** the **persistent** pro knows it is only a matter of time until the wheel turns again in his favor.

In addition to the previously mentioned way to **avoid** or **break** a sales slump, there are a few **other** tricks to the trade that may be your return ticket to high volume sales.

A. Make a **slight** change in the order of your presentation. This will prevent you from sounding **"too canned."**

B. Winners always **ask** for an order, they never **beg** for it. Sales people experiencing a slump tend to sell **too hard** and build up buyer resistence. "You can go to the table hungry, but never **starving."**

C. Make a **major** purchase you have been contemplating, such as a new car or a new wardrobe. This is a vote of **confidence** in yourself. When you **look** prosperous, you **feel** prosperous. Feeling better about **yourself** and your **future** is vital to turning a temporary setback into a stepping stone to success.

JUSTIFYING MARKETING INCENTIVES

Many, vacation resorts will contract with marketing companies who use various incentives with high **perceived** values to induce families to visit that particular resort.

A **credibility problem** often arises when the guests question the value of the incentive. A premium they **perceived** to have a value of several hundred dollars may, upon personal inspection, have a value of far less. Usually, the value is barely sufficient to compensate the guests for their time and travel.

Left unchecked, the **cynicism** caused by the dissappointment with the premium can spill over to the salesperson, the developer, the program and the product itself. Unless the quests believe the marketing methods are **legitimate** and **reasonable** , it is extremely difficult for the guests to believe in the value of your offer.

The salesperson **must** explain that premiums of modest value tend to **lower** the product **cost,** and this savings is passed on the the **owners.** By becoming an owner **today,** they can be assured of being a **big winner.**

CREATING URGENCY

How often have you heard someone say, "I bought that real estate **too soon?**" More often than not, people lament at all the missed opportunities they passed up. Since this is lifetime ownership, the sooner you act, the more benefits you will enjoy. The best time to start saving is **now.**

BUYERS ASSURANCE

Assure your buyers that you will not "love them and then leave them." Stress the fact you are a **career** professional and intend to be available for years to come to service their needs. Tell them you are very aware satisfied buyers refer their friends, and referrals are very important to your sales success.

THE TAKE-AWAY

When **hope of gain** does not motivate your guests to action, we can shift to **fear of loss,** better knows as the **"Take-away."**

When our guests do not respond well to all the benefits they will receive should they elect to join the program **(hope of gain)**, we can then shift to reminding them of all they will **lose (fear of loss)** by not becoming part of the program.

The "take-away" can be effectively applied in a number of ways:

A. Acknowledge they probably will not join today.

B. Explain your program "is not for everybody."

C. Adapt a certain air of independence — "We have thousands of **other** families in our market area who will appreciate our resort."

D. Once you have shifted to "fear of loss", speak of their opportunities in the **past** tense, not in the **future** tense.

Instead of saying:
"This is the pool your family **will** *enjoy."*
—Say
"This is the amount of savings you **could have** *realized today."*

Instead of saying:
"This is the amount of the savings you will realize today."
— Say
"This is the amount of savings you **could have** *realized today."*

By using — could have — would have — should have, you have **depressurized** your guests. You are **no longer selling,** merely going through the motions of explaining the many benefits your guests **would have** available to them **had** they elected to join.

The "take-away" can be made even more effective by inserting a few "urgency" statements, such as, "We expect to be completely sold out before . . . " or "This is the last unit we have at the **old** price. A price increase in scheduled to go into effect by . . . "

Once your guests start to respond to the "take-away", **do not pounce** on the **first** positive response. You catch a fish by first jiggling the bait to get his attention, then slowly **taking it away.** If you yank on the line at the first nibble, your fish will probably get away. You need more time for the fish to take the **whole** bait so that you can **set the hook.**

Help your guest "into the boat." Once the **fear** is overcome, they will enjoy the **ride!**

DON'T BE TOO REASONABLE

Very reasonable sales people tend to accept **any** reasonable excuse their guests give for not becoming involved in the program. The vast majority of guests legitimately have, or can quickly invent, **reasonable** excuses for not getting involved. In resort sales, it does not pay to be **too reasonable** when it comes to accepting excuses.

In a recent study of very successful sales professionals, the common denominator of the **top** sales **people** was a **fanatical belief** in their product. People with this degree of belief place so much **value** on their product that they refuse to accept or consider reasons why their guests should put their dollars **anywhere else.**

Sales people, in general, fell into one of the following four categories:

1. Doubted their product = **failure**

2. Liked their product = survival

3. Loved their product = do well

4. Fanatical about their product = #1

How do you **feel** about the product you are selling?

MAKE YOUR BUYER YOUR SALESPERSON

It is perfectly normal for the **proud** new buyers to tell their family, friends and co-workers about their recent purchase. They may also discuss the purchase with an accountant, attorney or financial advisor.

Any negative feedback to the buyers could result in rescission of the contract. Therefore, it is vitally important that **every** buyer be **well versed** in the logical and emotional reasons for the purchase. They must be able to relate fluently all the lifelong benefits to which they are now entitled.

When your buyers can **justify** their purchase, they will **prompt others** to buy. A happy, satisfied, well versed owner can be your **assistant** salesperson in the field. This is an **easy** way to increase your sales volume.

LOVE YOUR EARS, NOT YOUR MOUTH

When we **love our guests,** they feel the warmth of our friendship and genuine concern for their needs. Some sales people have **no room** in their hearts for their guests. Their **sole love** is the sound of their **own voice.** They talk incessantly, never **learning** anything new in the process.

If you **must** fall in love with a part of yourself, fall in love with your **ears.** They can earn **twice** the income your mouth can.

CUSTOMIZING THE PRESENTATION
TO YOUR GUESTS

The age, occupation, ethnic background and place of residence are major considerations when formulating the type of sales approach that should be used with the guests.

The general information of "nuts and bolts" in the presentation would **not** change from guest to guest, but how to **appeal to** or **motivate** each type of guest would vary greatly.

An entire **volume** could be devoted to this complex topic. The following is a very **brief sample** of some effective approaches. Only **uncommon sense** will tell you when to deviate or adjust for the many exceptions to these **general** guidelines.

SELLING BY AGES

Young — Motivated by:

A. Pride of ownership

B. Sense of independence

C. Forced savings

D. Providing for their Children

E. Opportunity for togetherness

Middle Aged — Motivated by:

A. Value

B. Status and prestige

C. Return on investment

D. Use and enjoyment

E. Opportunity for travel

Senior Citizens — Motivated by:

A. Trust and assurance

B. Health benefits

C. Rest and relaxation

D. **Safe** and **secure** investments

E. Legacy for children/grandchildren

SELLING BY ETHNIC BACKGROUND
Italians/Spanish - Emotional, family oriented.

Germans/Dutch - Analytical, logical. **Cleanliness** of resort is of above average importance.

Jewish - Judged by peers on basis of good **business sense.** Concentrate on value and bottom line.

Other Nationalities - Study the **values and customs** of each nationality. While exceptions do exist, the general **attitude** and **receptiveness** to your product will be **similar** for persons of a like ethnic heritage. **Sincerity** and **equal treatment** will get better results than being **patronizing.**

SELLING BY OCCUPATION
Chief Executive - Fast, professional presentation that gets quickly to the **bottom line.** Give **choices** so that top executive **feels** he is in **control.**

Bankers, Accountants, Engineers - Those who constantly work with figures require a **detailed** logical presentation, delivered in a slower, more deliberate manner. All the **technical** details must be **right** to motivate this **very** analytical group.

Professionals - Medical Doctors, Dentists, Attorneys-Status and a safe place to shelter income are prime motivators. The demands of their professions sometimes do not afford them ample time to research opportunities. Therefore, they base many of their decisions on the confidence they have in the salesperson. They **must perceive** the salesperson as another **highly skilled** and **knowledgeable professional.**

Educators - Conservative and preconditioned to "think about it" before acting. Peer pressure often prevents them from acting on their emotions. Educational travel opportunities and the more than average vacation time to enjoy all the **benefits** should be stressed. **Third party stories** about other educators who have joined can convince them to act **now.**

Blue Collar Workers - A simple, **emotional** presentation stressing the fun and excitement of quality vacations is all that is required. The forced savings and **long range** benefits should be stressed to build strong **commitment.** Without sufficient commitment, those with marginal incomes may **default** on their financial obligations.

Nurses - Capable and accustomed to making quick decisions. They know the dangers of excessive stress, and need an escape from the pressures of their profession. Be **positive** and **empathetic.**

Salespersons - The salesperson is not so much concerned about **buying** a **"bad deal"** as being **sold** a **"bad deal"** Treat him as an insider. Tell him you will dispense with the standard sales presentation. Then the salesperson will **feel** he **bought,** rather than was **sold.**

Plumbers, Electricians, Carpenters and other Skilled Craftsmen - Skilled craftsmen have above average income and will purchase easily, **provided** their current job offers some degree of **stability.**

Civil Service Workers - A security conscious conservative group. Many have traded a chance at the brass ring for a pension plan. The **safety** and **security** of your program, as well as the long range benefits and value, should be emphasized.

Farmers - Most farmers will plead poverty, but have more money buried in the barn than most other people have in the bank. They rely more on their common sense and natural intelligence as a guide than technical details. Their word is their bond and they seek others with the same moral standards.

Military Personnel - The possibility of transfer to another duty station often prevents them from setting down roots.

The advantage of having a vacation place, through the exchange service, available to them **whenever** they relocate is appealing. Those who do not own **any** real estate can be approached with this logical question "Doesn't it make sense to own at least a small piece of the country **you** are defending?"

Selling by Guests' place of Residence - Knowing something about the city, town or village where your guests reside can give you a good deal of insight ito the **lifestyle** and **priorities** of your guests. Do they live in an exclusive, posh area, a ghetto, or something in between. What type of social, cultural or recreational facilities does the area offer? The answer to these questions could just be the **edge** you need to close the sale.

RECIPROCITY

If you **confess** a fault to your guests, they are more willing to **confess** a fault to you.

If you first share information with your guests, they are more willing to share information with you.

If you occasionally respond, "I don't know, but I'll find out for you" — your guests will not feel intimidated or overwhelmed, and they will appreciate your honesty and sincere desire to help them.

If you **respond** thoughtfully to questions, rather than **react,** your guests will attach more credence to your answers.

If you **treat** your guests as buyers, they tend to rise to your level of expectations.

CHAPTER EIGHT

Customizing the Sales Presentation To Your Product

The professional salesperson is a merchant of words . To sell a different product, he merely changes **some** words. The **basic** sales principles and techniques remain the **same,** regardless of the product.

To provide the **cornerstone** for formulating a successful sales presentation for any type resort product, the sales trainer should **first** seek the answers to two key questions:

1. In what ways are the features and benefits of **my** product **superior** to those of resorts in my market area offering a **similar** vacation product?

2. What are the major benefits and advantages of **my** product, when compared to the various vacation **alternatives** available to the comparison shopper?

The answers to these **specific** questions will **isolate** the features, benefits and advantages of your resort product that are **superior** to those offered by competitors.

When the prospective buyer is convinced **your** positions of superiority are extremely significant in reaching a buying decision; most, if not all, the competition can be eliminated.

For instance, if your resort has the best **location,** then location should be **stressed** as one of the most important factors to consider in the purchase of your type product.

Are your prices **more reasonable?** Do you offer **better financing?** Is your resort more **accessible, cleaner, quieter,** safer? Are any of your recreation or social activities **superior?** Is the upkeep and maintenance of your product **less** than others? Do you have **more professional** owners services and follow-up? Is the **value,** or **resale value,** of your product **greater?** Does the **quality, size or performance** of your product **surpass** all others? Does it offer more **fun,** excitement, status? In what areas does it **more completely satisfy** the buyers' needs, wants and desires?

Virtually **every** resort or resort product has **at least one** position of superiority over its competitors. It is the job of the sales trainer to focus the presentation on areas that will afford the seller a **competitive edge.**

Each vacation alternative has its own **unique** position of superiority. For purposes of illustration, only a **few** of the countless assets of each vacation alternative can be listed in this text. However, with time, experience, and research, these suggested approaches can be altered, expanded and **customized** to suit **any** resort presentation.

The first vacation alternative we will consider is the **vacation homesite.**

Vacation Homesite - Superior to **other** type vacation alternatives because:

1. Land is not a **renewable** commodity - increased demand and diminishing supply have historically pushed **prices upward.**

2. Land does **not depreciate** (wear out) and requires **little maintenance** in its **natural** state.

3. **Land is an excellent legacy** to pass on to future generations.

COMPARISION TO OTHER
VACATION HOMESITE RESORTS

If Your resort is:
Closer to a major population area
Then Stress:
Convenience, easy access, **increased demand**

If your resort is:
Further from a major pupulation area
Then Stress:
Cleaner air - more scenic surroundings

If your resort is:
Near a major tourist area/attraction
Then Stress:
Area attraction

If your resort is:
Far from a major tourist area/attraction
Then Stress:
Resort activities

If your resort is:
Near major shopping and professional services
Then Stress:
Potential for conversion to primary or
retirement use

If your resort is:
Far from major shopping and professional services
Then Stress:
Vacation use

If your resort is:
Fully developed
Then Stress:
Immediate use and enjoyment

If your resort is:
In a preconstruction stage

Then Stress:
>   *Future use and probability of substantial prop-*
>   *erty value increases when fully developed.*

If your resort has:
>   Better pricing

Then Stress:
>   *Value*

If your resort has:
>   Better financing

Then Stress:
>   *Ease of ownership*

If your resort has:
>   **Paved private** roads

Then Stress:
>   *Exclusivity, access, value, less traffic*

If your resort has:
>   **Paved public** roads

Then Stress:
>   *No **direct** responsibility for road maintenance*

If your resort has:
>   **Unpaved** roads

Then Stress:
>   *Rustic, country charm, back to nature*

If your resort has:
>   **Better planning** or **zoning**

Then Stress:
>   *Protection and enhancement of property values*

If your resort has:
>   Better **protective covenants and restrictions**
>   on all construction

Then Stress:
>   *Peace of mind, developer guarantees, responsible*
control

If your resort has:
Exceptionally **large** properties
Then Stress:
   Low density — privacy

If your resort has:
Exceptionally **small** properties
Then Stress:
   Larger owner base to share expenses

STRESSING SPECIAL FEATURES

Each type vacation homesite has its own characteristics and is **superior** in some manner to all other homesites in that resort. Every buyer should feel there is some **special** feature or advantage to every homesite presented that would justify the purchase price.

If the homesite is:
Level
Then Stress:
   Easy access — Wider choice of building sites

If the homesite is:
Above road grade
Then Stress:
   Better drainage — Better views

If the homesite is:
Below road grade
Then Stress:
   Sheltered from elements — possible dramatic access from road via decking or ramps to second floor

If the homesite is:
Irregular in shape or terrain
Then Stress:
   "Architect" lot - Most potential for creativity

If the homesite is:
Sloped

Then Stress:
> *Less excavation for full basement — lends itself to terracing and multilevel decking*

If the homesite is:
Sloped
Then Stress:
> *Less excavation for full basement — lends itself to terracing and multilevel decking*

If the homesite is:
Sparcely wooded
Then Stress:
> *Lowers clearing costs — Select own plantings — Easily adaptable for gardening*

If the homesite is:
Heavily wooded
Then Stress:
> *Seclusion — Shade*

If the homesite is:
Bedrock
Then Stress:
> *Solid foundation*

If the homesite is:
Sandy
Then Stress:
> ***Easy*** *excavation — Good absorption*

If the homesite is:
Mostly hardwoods
Then Stress:
> *Summer shade — Vibrant colors in Fall*

If the homesite is:
Mostly **evergreens**
Then Stress:
> *Green year round — Clean refreshing scent*

If the homesite is:
Complete with **central water** and **sewerage**
Then Stress:
Savings on cost of on-site well and septic system reliability and guarantee of supply

If the homesite is:
Not supplied with water and sewerage

Then Stress:
Private supply of *quality* chemical free well water
Independence — not subject to constantly increasing utility bills

If the homesite is:
On a **hilltop**
Then Stress:
Panoramic views — Cool breezes

If the homesite is:
In the **valley**
Then Stress:
Sheltered from elements, more fertile soil

If the homesite is:
On the **waterfront**
Then Stress:
High value — Private dock, private lake access

If the homesite is:
In the **interior**
Then Stress:
Less humidity — quieter

If the homesite is:
Near recreation facilities
Then Stress:
Convenience

If the homesite is:
Walking distance from facilities

Then Stress:
  Short **walk** — *good for health*

If the homesite is:
  Far from facilities
Then Stress:
  Short **drive** — *away from noise and crowds*

The second vacation alternative to be analyzed is the **vacation home.**

An infinite variety of styles, prices, and sizes are available. In recent years, townhouses and condominiums have gained in popularity. Previously, the second home market had consisted almost totally of one family detached homes, of rustic or conventional design.

Vacation home purchasers are seldom influenced by lower priced alternatives. Their first priority would be to satisfy a need or want for more privacy, prestige, status or space. Those with large families often prefer to **own,** rather than rent.

Vacation home purchasers are also willing to tolerate a higher annual cash outlay in the belief their equity build-up in inflationary increases in the resale value of the second home will return most of their investment, and possibly a **profit** as well.

Due to the substantial amount of dollars involved in the purchase and upkeep of a second home, the buyer **expects** the salesperson to be knowledgeable about a wide variety of subjects which relate to the home.

Success in selling vacation homes is more reliant on expert **product knowledge** than most other vacation alternatives.

Having the answers to the following questions will give you the edge needed.

How does the prices, per square foot of living area, for your homes compare to the competition?

If your prices are higher, can you **easily** justify the difference?

Are your styles and design in line with current market demand trends?

Do you offer any **special** features in your homes not available elsewhere?

Are your building materials more durable? Do you use brand names? Are your designs more functional, practical or dramatic? If your workmanship superior?

Is the home easily maintained and energy efficient?

On existing homes, can you customize or enlarge homes to suit the buyers' needs?

On new construction, can you deliver a finished home within promised time frames? Can your competitors?

Are your **guarantees** or **follow-up** superior to the competition?

Are real estate taxes or homeowners insurance rates in your area lower than average?

Are other annual costs such as maintenance fees, community dues and facility use fees lower than average for the area?

Is security protection, police, fire and medical services available on site or nearby?

What type of social or cultural environment does the area offer?

What is the proximity to area schools, churches, shopping and professional services?

SALES AND MARKETING

What special bonuses or incentives does the developer/-builder offer to motivate the prospective buyer to act **today?** Do they compare favorably with the competition?

Is your advertising budget sufficient to generate enough propsects to meet sales goals?

Is your sales force well versed to answer most of the common questions potential second home buyers may have?

Is your financing competitive?

What has been the resale potential and annual rate of appreciation for homes in your area?

The previous questions will **isolate** one or more areas your vacation homes are superior to the competition. Build your presentation around that **competitive edge.**

The third major vacation alternative is **camping.**

Some of the major advantages of **camping,** when compared to other vacation alternatives are:

Lower Costs - Although top of the line motorized homes can easily **exceed** the cost of the average vacation home, the vast majority of campers select lower cost, affordable options.

The cost of cooking out over a campfire can be **less** than the **tips** one would give in a posh restaurant.

Variety and Mobility - From pitching a tent in the wilderness, to parking a recreational vehicle on a shared or wholly owned campsite in a trailer park, literally thousands of combinations are possible.

No other vacation alternative can match the **mobility** of camping. Put the camper body on the back of the pick-up truck, or hitch the pop-up camper to the family car. Try a sleek fifth wheel travel trailer or hook-up to an aerodynamically designed model, containing more luxury features than found in many homes. Something is available to suit every lifestyle.

Lower Upkeep - The cost of maintaining the average camper is far less than the annual cost of maintaining a second home. The annual real estate taxes and insurance premiums on a vacation home alone might well exceed the total cost of the camping.

Closer to Nature - All monetary considerations aside, camping provides a refreshing change from the pressures of modern society. A walk in the woods, a breath of fresh air, a scenic view, a roaring campfire, or relaxing under a starry sky, restores body and soul.

The **fourth** major **vacation alternative** is **vacation time-sharing.**

The vacation unit is fully furnished and then divided into fifty two weekly increments. One or two weeks are set aside for maintenance purposes. The remainder are sold in weekly intervals.

Each family purchases one or more weeks, paying only for the time and space they occupy. An annual maintenance fee is paid that covers the pro rata share of the cost of maintaining the unit, the common area and facilities.

Timesharing has undergone numerous dramatic changes since its inception. Literally hundreds of different sales methods and product variations exist between the thousands of timeshare resorts now in existence.

Explaining the differences between seasons, right to use and deeded resorts, quartershares, exchange services, unit sizes and types, purpose built and renovated home and destination resorts and dozens of other variations within the timeshare industry, is best left to the on-site trainer.

This text will only highlight the **positions of superiority** each vacation alternative possesses, in order to illustrate how an effective competitive presentaion can be made for **every** resort product.

The **advantages** of timesharing, when compared to its **main** competitor, the **resort** hotel and motel are:

Timeshare units are generally **more spacious** and **luxurious** than the average hotel room.

Kitchen facilities in timeshare units offer **convenience** and **substantial savings** on vacation food costs.

Leasing or owning a timeshare unit **eliminates hotel reservation hassles.**

Purchasing a timeshare unit at a one time **fixed** price provides an excellent **hedge against inflation.** Hotel and motel rates have steadily increased at an annual rate substantially higher than the overall rate of inflation.

Social functions and recreational facilities at most timeshare resorts are either included in the maintenance fees or offered to members at discounted rates.

The timeshare vacationer who is also a member of a vacation exchange service enjoys many **fringe benefits,** such as discounted airfares and car rental, vacation magazines., annual directories, and detailed descriptions of all amenities at member resorts.

Money paid for hotel and motel rooms is **spent** and non recoverable. The owner of a **deeded** timeshare receives **ownership** and an **opportunity** to build **equity.** Under ideal circumstances, the timeshare owner could realize a **return** of most, if not all, of their investment, upon resale of the **deed.**

The major advantages of timeshare when compared to the vacation home are:

Timesharing provides a luxurious vacation at a **fraction of the cost** of a vacation home.

Many of the **worries** and expense of the second home owner are alleviated or minimized for the timeshare vacationer.

Security, management, maintenance, complete furishing, replacement of furnishing, utilities and main service are all included in the timeshare annual maintenance fee.

The vacation home is in one **fixed location,** but the timeshare vacationer, who is a member of an exchange service, can exchange his unit for others in a wide **variety of locations.**

The major advantages of timesharing when compared to **camping** are:

The timeshare vacationer enjoys more privacy, luxury and spaciousness than the average camper. Jacuzzis and color cable TV are common in the timeshare units, but rare in recreation vehicles.

Timesharing provides shelter from the elements and insects, often a problem for the camper.

Timesharing offers many **conveniences** not readily available to **campers.** For instance, campers are usually more limited in the variety of food that can be properly prepared, without a fully-equipped kitchen at their disposal.

Recreational vehicles are limited to continental United States and only those countries accessible by road.

On the other hand, the timeshare vacationer often flies worldwide to the destination of their choice.

Despite the advantages listed above, it is **far easier** to convince the **avid** camper to **supplement** his current vacation lifestyle with a week or two of luxury timeshare vacations, than to recommend he change his vacation lifestyle **totally.**

Some less than avid campers chose that lifestyle because it appeared to be the **only affordable** way to vacation. For those who fit this category, **start them out** with your **most affordable** timeshare week.

In summary, whatever your vacation product may be, **isolate** the positions of superiority **your** product enjoys when compared to similar products or other alternatives. The best way to **beat** the competition is to **eliminate** the competition, at lease in the mind of your guests.

CHAPTER NINE

Management

Recruiting, Hiring and Promoting Practices

People are the most important resource of any business. The best planning, the best product and the best financing will **not** assure success, if the **people** involved lack the talent and dedication to get the job done.

In **theory**, therefore, the resort developer should strive to recruit the best available talent at the **top** level, thus setting a high standard of selectivity and excellence that would filter down through the ranks.

In **reality,** however, ideal hiring standards are often subordinated to ego gratification, company politics and individual protectionism.

An **awareness** of these potential pitfalls is helpful in recruiting, maintaining and promoting competent personnel at all levels.

Some of the most **common** problems encountered in organizing an effective sales force include:

1. On all levels, the tendency is to hire or promote persons who most closely **mirror** the person doing the hiring. Whether a candidate for a position agrees with the views of the interviewer or flatters their ego should **not** be the **primary** consideration in the selection process. The **qualifications** and **competence** for the position in question should be the sole criteria. Beware of the **clone** maker.

2. Manpower needs should be analyzed and **anticipated** as far

in **advance** as possible. Waiting until the manpower shortage is **critical,** results in **"hiring by crisis."** All standards are thrown to the wind in the rush to fill vacancies. Allow ample time to be **selective.**

3. **Insecurity** often prompts people to surround themselves with less competent subordinates who pose no threat to their position. Make sure your "Superstars" are not impeded in their rise to the top by those who feel threatened.

4. Do not promote anyone **solely** on the basis of outstanding performance in their **present** position. The most outstanding **sales persons** may make the worst **sales managers.** Evaluate each candidate for the **qualifications** needed for the next step up. It is far better to **increase** the **compensation** for management and salespeople who are doing outstanding work, than to **reward** them with a promotion to a level beyond their abilities.

The following section provides **guidelines** for recruiting an **effective** sales team. The competent professional sales manager and trainer can **mold** rookies into sales professionals, **provided** they have the proper raw material from the start. Putting extreme pressure on a lump of coal for a few **million** years might create a **diamond.** however, if you wish to create a polished brilliant diamond within a **short** time span, you must start with a "diamond in the rough."

RECRUITING THE SALES FORCE

Anticipate manpower needs **in advance.**

Allow sufficient time to be **selective.**

Use first class locations for recruiting.

Use large ads to get better results.

Identify best areas for recruiting and concentrate effort on those areas.

Recruit large numbers of applicants through organized campaigns.

Use a variety of methods and media to recruit.

Offer incentives to sales staff to generate candidates for sales positions.

Have employment applications **fully completed** before start of interview.

Use group presentation methods to **screen** large numbers of applicants, followed by **personal** interviews.

Generate at least two applicants for every position to be filled.

Know the favorable traits and characteristics most likely to enhance applicants chances for a successful sales career.

Be objective.

Check references and past employment history.

Eliminate applicants with traits that would not blend with the climate and culture of your organization.

Seek out those with a strong desire to succeed and a willingness to learn.

Highlight why people are **proud** to be associated with your company.

Point out past track record, objectives, goals, and growth of the firm.

Clearly define expectations and standards of the industry.

Spell out working schedule, compensation, benefits, and career opportunities.

Give a **detailed** job description.

List commitments company will make to ensure applicant's success.

Give basic written exam to test comprehension, common sense and trainability of applicants.

Interview all applicants at least **twice.**

Only make promises and commitments the company will stand behind.

Hire a balanced group of people.

Share surplus applications with other departments.

SALES TRAINING

The **effective** sales manager **must** be able to understand and relate well to a variety of personality types. In order to **motivate** a sales line, the manager must know exactly what makes **each** salesperson tick.

Many sales people look to their manager as a **role model.** For this group, the manager **must** lead by **example. Show** them how, don't just **tell** them how.

For those that are very **competitive,** provide competition. For the **followers,** be an excellent leader. For the **leaders,** give them enough freedom to exercise their **creativity.**

For the **family oriented** salespeople, **involve** the family. Social functions and vacation awards that include the **whole** family will keep that salesperson stimulated at home as well as at work.

The **theorists** constantly resists the way things **are,** and devotes most of their time verbalizing or planning how things would be, if **they** were running the show. The theorists can be handled with the logic they must **conform** and **perform** above average in order to rise to a level in the company where they could implement their own ideas.

Other personality types range from the **total professional,** who requires only support and recognition, to the **con artist,** who must be weeded out as quickly as possible.

Upbeat sales meetings and high quality sales training are useful to motivate the sales line on a whole, but they are effective **only** in **conjunction** with **one** on **one** attention to **every** person on the sales line.

Upper Management
The top management should concentrate on the overall sales **plan** and establishing company **policy. (What** must be done.)

POLICY MANUAL
A manual clearly stating company policy must be accessible to all salespeople. **Changes** in policy should be prominently posted and the policy manual kept current.

Policy, to be effective, must be enforced fairly and uniformly. **Everyone** should abide by the **chain of command.** Allow neither **prima donnas** nor **victims.**

Middle Management
Middle management should concentrate on establishing **procedure. (When** and **where** it should be done.)

LINE RULES AND REGULATIONS
Most are willing to play the game if they know the rules.

A clear, concise, uniformly applied list of Line Rules and Regulations should be provided to every new trainee, plus be posted in a conspicuous place.

Reporting times, dress code, vehicle maintenance, attendance, line rotation and penalties for non-compliance are but a few of the major items that must be clearly stated in the **LINE RULES AND REGULATIONS.**

Line Management
The line managers should concentrate on sales and sales instruction. (**How** to do it.)

General Management Guidelines
Statistics should be your servant, not your **master.** Let common sense prevail.

First be **effective,** then concentrate on how to be more **efficient.**

Anything worth doing is worth the time for proper planning.

Move quickly on decisions that can be reversed, and more slowly and deliberately on irreversible decisions.

Start with **tight** control, then loosen control as a vote of confidence when desired objectives and goals are being obtained.

Handle problems one at a time. Rank by category and severity. Short term problems and those with the greatest impact on profits should be given first priority.

Give key personnel a financial interest in the success of the company. Better to reward and build around them, than to end up in competition with them.

During slow periods, rotate staff to perform more than one function. Minimize total reliance on any one individual.

The happy medium in projecting the proper future course of the company usually lies somewhere **between** the recommendations of the ultra conservative "charts and graphs" business manager and the "fly by the seat of your pants" entrepreneur.

Words of Wisdom

Be Likeable - People **listen** to those who are likeable, and **when** they **pay attention, they are more apt to buy.**

Perfect practice makes perfect - **Role play** or **practice** only when a **highly skilled professional** is on hand to critique your performance. Dialogue between two **unskilled, unsupervised** trainees **reinforces errors.**

Wealth is determined by what we **save,** not by what we **earn.**

YES!! Virtually everything in life we possess, of **worth** or **value,** we oftained by saying **yes.**

Objections are **magnified** by opposition and **minimized** by agreement.

Cynics don't listen — establish **credibility before** your product presentation.

When guests ask the **time,** don't tell them how to build a watch! (K.I.S.S.)

Flexible people do not get bent out of shape.

The salesperson must know **much more** to **sell** than each **buyer** must know in order **to buy.**

Prepare for tomorrow by performing **today.**

When you stop **learning** more, you stop **earning** more. Ignorance is **more expensive** than education.

Sales techniques that gain **compliance,** without instilling **commitment,** will not produce a **satisfied** buyer.

Compliance is the **building block** of the sale, but **commitment** is the mortar that holds the sale together and gives it durability.

People buy what they **want,** quicker than what they **need.**

A pound of **conviction** is worth a **ton** of **logic.**

Warm people **benefits** sell more than cold hard **facts.**

It is better to pay a little **more** than you **expected** than a little **less** than you **should.**

You can't **climb** the ladder of success with your hands in your **pockets.**

There are no **small** sales — the forest of mighty oaks started with just **one** acorn.

The **"toughest"** sale is the best teacher.

The will that weakens **first,** strengthens the other one.

The evasive guest will try to **substitute compliments** for **commitment.**

Every sale should start between the salesperson's ears **before** he meets his guests.

The husband is the **king** of the castle, but his wife is the **treasurer.**

The husband is the **head** of the family, but the wife is the **neck** that **turns** the **head.**

The **source** of spectacular performance is **commitment** and **preparation.**

The mind is like an umbrella. It only works when it's **open.**

People want to **learn,** but resist being **taught.**

If you hit a home run, but fail to touch all the bases, you're **still out.**

The game is won by the team with the least **errors.**

Answer **logical** objections with **emotion,** and answer **emotional** objections with **logic.**

Tangibles give your guests a **reason** to buy.

Intangibles give your guests an **excuse** to buy.

Sometimes, we can't see the **forest** for the **trees.**

We never learn anything **new** while we are **talking.**

Selling is the art of **persuasion** to obtain agreement, not **intimidation** to obtain **compliance.**

God gave us **two ears** and only **one mouth.** LISTEN more than you **speak.**

What you **do** with what you know is more important than what you know.

Losers replace buyers. Winners **maintain** and **add** new buyers.

People don't **care** how much you know, until they **know** how much you **care.**

Increase the **productive** time you spend either selling or in preparation for sales, and you automatically increase sales.

"Better a late accounting of the **profits,** than a timely accounting of the **losses.**"

"Selling contributes to **profits.** Everything else contributes to **costs.**"

"Do not engage mouth until you have put your brain in motion."

Within a sales organization. only sales contribute to **profits.** All other departments contribute to **costs.** Give your salespeople the respect and recognition they **deserve.**

— The End —

QUALITY TRAINING PROGRAM
Q.T. TESTS

1. Review the list of words on the numbered word list.

2. For each question, insert the **Number** of the **most appropriate** word(s).

3. Circle numbers on word list as numbers are used. The same word can only be used in **one** place, **except** words that appear more than once on work list.

4. Upon completion, check test answers against answer sheets.

Grading

2 points for each correct answer

2 points deducted for **no** answer (blank).

3 points deducted for incorrect answers.

The time allotted for each test is 40 minutes.

EXAMPLE:	**Answer Number**
1. The sun is _____	2.
2. An elephant is _____	3.

TEST WORDS

1.	Blue	3.	Large
2.	Yellow	4.	Small

Q.T TEST 1 WORDS

1. Act
2. Advantage
3. Agreement
4. Approval & Reassurance
5. Benefits
6. Bottom Line
7. Cancellations
8. Common bond
9. Cost
10. Credibility
11. Cynicism
12. Detail
13. Dissertation
14. Doubt
15. Emotions
16. Empathy
17. Expectations
18. Fanatical
19. Fast
20. Fear
21. Finesse
22. For
23. Found
24. Gain
25. Health & Happiness
26. If I could, would you
27. Ignored
28. Intangible
29. Isolate
30. Isolated
31. Know
32. Legacy
33. Mental Pauses
34. Motive
35. Optimist
36. Overcome
37. Patronize
38. Prejudge
39. Pride of ownership
40. Reciprocity
41. Return on Investment
42. Safety & Security
43. Slow
44. Superiority
45. Suppose
46. Tangible
47. Tell
48. Think
49. To
50. Total
51. Use & Enjoyment
52. Value
53. Yourself
54. Zeal

1. The most important person you can sell is _____

2. You should never show a **feature** of your resort without explaining the _____ to your guests at the same time.

3. An **advantage** your resort offers that is not found at most other resorts, is known as a position of _____

4. When guests first raise minor objections, they usually should be _____

5. Major objections, and minor objections raised repeatedly, you should first _____ the objection before trying to overcome it.

6. Once the objection has been _____ you should then _____ the objection.

7. **One word** that can be used to separate excuses from valid reasons is _____

8. **One phrase** that can be used to separate excuses from valid reasons is _____

9. The most important **investment** your guests can make is an investment in their _____ and _____

10. Selling past the close creates _____ in the mind of the buyer.

11. **Fear and apprehension** of the buyer, after the sale, leads to _____ of the contract.

12. **Logic** causes your guests to _____

13. **Emotion** causes your guests to _____

14. Salespeople who believe in their product, feel they are doing something _____ the buyer, rather than doing something _____ the buyer.

15. _____ all you tell, don't _____ all you know.

16. When quoting costs to your guests, **first** give the _____ amount required, **then** itemize all the items that are **included.**

17. I know how you **feel**. I've **felt** that way myself. But once I looked into the matter thoroughly I _____ it was no problem. _____

18. Quality items that have a **higher price,** often _____ **less** in the long run. _____

19. You can avoid a non-stop sales presentation by giving your guests _____ _____ at frequent intervals during the presentation. _____

20. When your guests question the honesty and sincerity of your presentation, you have a _____ problem. _____

21. It is important to establish **credibility** at the **beginning** of any presentation to overcome any _____ _____

22. Selling can be broken down into two major categories. Hope of _____ _____ of loss. _____

23. The **top salespeople** in every field are usually _____ about their product. _____

24. **Young people** are most easily motivated by _____ _____

25. **Middle age people** are most easily motivated by _____ _____

26. **Senior citizens** are most easily motivated by _____ _____

27. **Minority members** respond better to sincerity and equal treatment than being _____ _____

28. An agressive top **executive** would prefer a _____ presentation, quickly getting to the _____ _____

29. An **analytical type** would prefer a _____ presentation containing much _____ _____

30. An outgoing, **extroverted** fun loving person would be more likely to purchase based upon their _____ rather than logic. _____

31. A laid back, easy going family oriented person would probably wish to seek _____ and _____ from their family. _____

32. If you treat your guests as **buyers,** they tend to rise to your level of _____ _____

33. When you share information about **yourself** to your guests, they are more willing to share information about themselves. This is the principle of psychological _____   _____

34. A more favorable position is an _____   _____

35. An understanding between two or more people is an _____   _____

36. Something in common that tends to unite is a _____   _____

37. A lengthy discourse on some subject is a _____   _____

38. Ability to share in another's emotion and actions is _____   _____

39. The ability to handle **difficult** situations skillfully and diplomatically is _____   _____

40. That which **cannot** be touched — having no form or substance is _____   _____

41. That which **can** be touched — having form and substance is _____   _____

42. Some **inner** drive that causes a person to do something or act in a certain way is a _____   _____

43. One who expects the **best** possible outcome in any circumstances is an _____   _____

44. To judge beforehand **without** all the **facts** is to _____   _____

Q.T. TEST 2 WORDS

1.	Active	29.	Magnified
2.	Alternative	30.	Minimized
3.	Alternatives	31.	Most
4.	Assumptive	32.	Needs
5.	Battle	33.	Own
6.	Ben Franklin	34.	Pact
7.	Body Language	35.	Perspiration
8.	Breaks	36.	Persuasion
9.	Commitment	37.	Procrastination
10.	Credibility	38.	Professional
11.	Demand	39.	Question
12.	Discretionary	40.	Rate
13.	Do	41.	Rearranging
14.	Equity	42.	Reinforce
15.	Exchange	43.	Responsively
16.	Face	44.	Sell
17.	Facts	45.	Summary
18.	Freewill	46.	Tact
19.	Goals & Objectives	47.	Tantalizer
20.	Graphics	48.	Temperature
21.	Harmonize	49.	Third
22.	Inflation	50.	Value
23.	Intent	51.	Wants
24.	Larger	52.	Watch
25.	Least	53.	War
26.	Listen	54.	Win/Win
27.	Location		
28.	Logic		

1. Delicate perception of the right thing to say or do is _____   _____

2. One who does something with great **skill** is _____   _____

3. The degree of **usefulness, importance, desirability** which anything is **thought** of being worth is _____   _____

4. To establish faith, confidence, or belief in **oneself** is to _____   _____

5. When you give your guests a choice between two **positive** alternatives, this is know as the _____ choice close _____   _____

6. Making a side by side list of the pros and cons of any matter and deciding pro or con based upon which list is longer, is known as the _____ close.   _____

7. Proceeding to fill out a worksheet/purchase order, **without** receiving a firm verbal commitment to purchase, on the positive assumption your guests **will** buy, is know as an _____ close.   _____

8. Summing up all the **benefits** and advantages of your product, just before asking for the order, is known as a _____ close.   _____

9. You should **never** argue with your guests. Always _____ with their objections.   _____

10. When you argue with your guests, you may **win** the _____ but you will **lose** the _____   _____

11. Once we have satisfied our basic **needs,** the "spice of life" is when we satisfy our _____   _____

12. The value of a property beyond the amount owed is the _____   _____

13. The most important feature of real estate that determines value is _____   _____

14. Prices of real estate are effected by the law of supply and _____   _____

15. A sudden drop in the value of money and a rise in prices is called _____   _____

16. You can lower guests **tension** upon arrival by telling them your _____   _____

17. Before arriving at a resort, many guests make a _____ not to purchase under any circumstances.   _____

18. You have _____ when your sales statements are accepted as true fact.   _____

19. To determine our guests' vacation preferences, we should always ask what they liked _____ and _____ about their last vacation.   _____

20. The salesperson should listen intently, selectively and _____   _____

21. When unsure of the motive for a question asked, you should answer the question **with** a _____   _____

22. Thomas Edison defined **genius** as 1% inspiration and 99% _____   _____

23. Communication is an _____ of information.   _____

24. We communicate three ways, verbally, tone of voice and _____   _____

25. Adjust the _____ of your presentation to suit the capacity of your guests to absorb information.   _____

26. We should not **compete** with our guests. We should convey to them that our offer is a _____ situation.   _____

27. We should **help** out guests solve their problems and achieve their _____   _____

28. Any **written** figures we wish to stress should be written _____ than all other figures.   _____

29. Charts, drawings and printed materials used to **document** sales claims are called _____   _____

30. A statement used to **peak** your customer's interest is called a _____ statement.   _____

31. When your guests say no to your offer, they are saying yes to less desirable _____   _____

32. Using "tie downs" will help to gain agreement and _____ _____

33. Trial closes are a way to take your guests' _____ _____

34. "In which bedroom will the children be sleeping? — is an example of an _____ question. _____

35. Don't tell your guests what something **is** — tell them what **it can** _____ for them. _____

36. Income **not** already committed to other obligations is known as _____ income. _____

37. When you tell your guests a story about another couple, **just like them,** who are now owners at your resort, you would be telling a _____ party story. _____

38. Selling is a matter of _____ your guests priorities. _____

39. Adding **new** information, after your guests have said **no** to your offer, gives them a _____ saving way to say **yes.** _____

40. Imperfect, unsupervised practice only tends to _____ errors. _____

41. Objections are _____ by opposition and _____ by agreement. _____

42. When your guests ask for the **time,** don't tell them how to build a _____ _____

43. A **pound** of conviction is worth a **ton** of _____ _____

44. Warm people **benefit** sell more than cold hard _____ _____

45. Selling is the act of _____ to obtain agreement, not intimidation to gain compliance. _____

46. We have *two* ears and only **one** mouth. We should _____ twice as much as we talk. _____

ANSWERS

Q.T. TEST 1

1. 53 Yourself
2. 5 Benefits
3. 44 Superiority
4. 27 Ignored
5. 29 Isolate
6. 30 Isolated
   36 Overcome
7. 45 Suppose
8. 26 If I could, would you
9. 25 Health & Happiness
10. 14 Doubt
11. 7 Cancellation
12. 48 Think
13. 1 Act
14. 22 For
    49 to
15. 31 Know
    47 Tell
16. 50 Total
17. 23 Found
18. 9 Cost
19. 33 Mental Pauses
20. 10 Credibility
21. 11 Cynicism
22. 24 Gain
    20 Fear
23. 18 Fanatical
24. 25, 26 A choice of
    39 Pride of Ownership
    41 Return on Investment
    51 Use & Enjoyment
    42 Safety & Security
    32 Legacy
27. Patronized
28. 19 Fast
    6 Bottom Line
29. 43 Slow
    12 Detail
30. 15 Emotions
31. 4 Approval &
    Reassurance
32. 17 Expectations
33. 40 Reciprocity
34. 2 Advantage
35. 3 Agreement
36. 8 Common Bond
37. 13 Dissertation
38. 16 Empathy
39. 21 Finesse
40. 28 Intangible
41. 46 Tangible
42. 34 Motive
43. 35 Optimist
44. 38 Prejudge

Q.T. TEST 2

1. 46 Tact
2. 38 Professional
3. 50 Value
4. 44 Sell
5. 2 Alternate
6. 6 Ben Franklin
7. 4 Assumptive
8. 45 Summary
9. 21 Harmonize
10. 5 Battle
    53 War
11. 51 Wants
12. 14 Equity
13. 27 Location
14. 11 Demand
15. Inflation
16. 23 Intent
17. 34 Pact
    8 Breaks
18. 10 Credibility
19. 31 Most
    25 Least
20. 43 Responsively
21. 39 Question
22. 35 Perspiration
23. 15 Exchange
24. 7 Body Language
25. 40 Rate
26. 54 Win/Win
27. 19 Goals & Objectives
28. 24 Larger
29. 20 Graphics
30. 47 Tantalizer
31. 3 Alternatives
32. 9 Commitment
33. 48 Temperature
34. 1 Active
35. 13 Do
36. 12 Discretionary
37. 49 Third
38. 41 Rearranging
39. 16 Face
40. 42 Reinforce
41. 29 Magnified
    30 Minimized
42. 52 Watch
43. 28 Logic
44. 17 Facts
45. 36 Persuasion
46. 26 Listen

INDEX

... ORDER FORM ...

The Art & Science of Resort Sales

If you need additional copies of *The Art & Science of Resort Sales,* simply call us toll free or mail the handy order form today! All orders are rushed within 24 hours of your order!

1 to 9 copies $19.95
10 to 49 copies $15.96
50 or more copies . . . . .Call for Discounts

Shipping/Handling $3.20 for 1st copy, $1.00 for each additional copy. Ten (10) or more copies add 4% shipping and handling.

Call Toll Free
800-248-3555
Ask for Operator #623
(Outside U.S. call: (530) 622-7777

Name _____

Company _____

Address _____

C/S/Z _____

Day Phone ( )_____

Please send me:_____copies at $ _____each

Sub Total _____

7¼% Tax (Calif. only)_____

Shipping/Handing_____

TOTAL _____

☐ Visa   ☐ Mastercard   ☐ American Express   ☐ Discover   ☐ Check

Card Number_____

Expiration_____Signature_____

Mail Order to:
Hampton Books
P.O. Box 2481 Dept. #623
Placerville, CA 95667-2481
United States

AS NATIONALLY ADVERTISED

The
Closers

This is the famous *Blue Book* that can put you at the top of the highest paid profession in the world — Professional Sales! This is the most famous and powerful book on closing sales ever written! Become Master Closer with the *Secret Blue Book* that can *Double* — even *Triple* your income!

300 pg. Book..$24.95

Audio Program..$99.95

... Quantity Discounts are Available ...

Call Toll Free
800-248-3555
Ask for Operator #623
(Outside U.S. call: (530) 622-7777

Name_____

Company_____

Address_____

C/S/Z_____

Day Phone (   )_____

Please send me:

☐ *Book*   ☐ *Audio Program*

Sub Total_____

7¼% Tax (Calif. only)_____

Shipping/Handing_____

TOTAL_____

☐ Visa ☐ Mastercard ☐ American Express ☐ Discover ☐ Check

Card Number_____

Expiration_____Signature_____

Mail Order to:
Hampton Books
P.O. Box 2481 Dept. #623
Placerville, CA 95667-2481
United States